Chris Podwysocki and **Gail Johnson** met in 1989 on the island of Koh Samui where they ran a small beach bar for two years. Prior to that, they each began travelling in their teens and between them have lived in and visited various parts of western and eastern Europe, the USA and Mexico, Asia, South-east Asia, Australia and the Pacific and, most recently, North-west Africa.

Currently Chris and Gail are living in Dulwich, London, where they are taking a temporary break between travels to await the arrival of a new member of the family.

Acknowledgements

We would like to say thank you to all the travellers who spent time with us at our bar "Bodgett and Scarper" that we had on the island and all the people who helped out at the start.

Without them we could not have spent the time we did on Koh Samui which enabled us to write this book.

We would also like to thank the Thai Tourist Board for their co-operation.

(Front cover) *One of the numerous ferry boats that take visitors around the islands, with the typically lush green vegetation of Koh Samui in the background.*

KOH SAMUI
Gulf of Thailand

PARADISE FOUND

A TOUR AROUND
A TROPICAL ISLAND

Chris Podwysocki and Gail Johnson

Roger Lascelles, Cartographic and Travel Publisher
47 York Road, Brentford, Middlesex TW8 OQP. Tel: 081 847 0935

Publication Data

Title Koh Samui, Gulf of Thailand
Photographs Chris Podwysocki and Gail Johnson and the Thai Tourist Board
Maps John Gill, Chessington, Surrey
Printing Stamford Press Ptd Ltd, 48 Lorong 21, Singapore 1438
ISBN 0 903909 97 9
Edition First September 1992
Publisher Roger Lascelles
47 York Road, Brentford, Middlesex, TW8 OQP
Copyright Chris Podwysocki and Gail Johnson

Distribution

Africa:	South Africa	—	Faradawn, Box 17161, Hillbrow 2038
Americas:	Canada	—	International Travel Maps and Books, P.O. Box 2290, Vancouver BC V6B 3W5
	U.S.A.	—	Available through major booksellers with good foreign travel sections
Asia:	India	—	English Book Store, 17-L Connaught Circus, P.O. Box 328, New Delhi 110 001
Australasia:	Australia	—	Rex Publications, 15 Huntingdon Street, Crows Nest, N.S.W.
Europe:	Belgium	—	Brussels — Peuples et Continents
	Germany	—	Available through major booksellers with good foreign travel sections
	GB/Ireland	—	Available through all booksellers with good foreign travel sections
	Italy	—	Libreria dell'Automobile, Milano
	Netherlands	—	Nilsson & Lamm BV, Weesp
	Denmark	—	Copenhagen — Arnold Busck, G.E.C., Gad, Boghallen
	Finland	—	Helsinki — Akateeminen Kirjakauppa
	Norway	—	Oslo — Arne Gimnes/J.G Tanum
	Sweden	—	Stockholm/Esselte, Akademi Bokhandel, Fritzes, Hedengrens Gothenburg/Gumperts, Esselte Lund/Gleerupska
	Switzerland	—	Basel/Bider; Berne/Atlas; Geneve/Artou; Lausanne/Artou; Zurich/Travel Bookshop

Contents

1 Introducing Koh Samui 7
Location and physical features 9 — Seasons: when
to go 10 — What to take 10 — Documentation 11 —
Money 11

2 How to get there 13
From Bangkok: direct 13 — From Surat Thani:
by ferry 14

3 The island and its people 17
Historical background 17 — The people 18 —
Religion 18 — Customs 20 — Festivals 21

4 Transport 22
Taxis 22 — Vehicle hire 22 — Petrol stations 24

5 Accommodation 25
Bungalows 25 — Self-catering accommodation 26 —
Hotels 26

6 Food and drink 27
The Thai diet 27 — Some Thai delicacies 28 —
Fruit 29 — A handful of restaurants 29 — Drinks 32
—Bars 33

7 Naton 35
Amenities in Naton 35 — Shopping 37 — Eating
out 38 — Accommodation 38

8 Beaches and sea 40
Chaweng beach 40 — Lamai beach 41 — Other
beaches 41 — The sea 41

9 Sightseeing 43
Waterfalls 43 — Samui Highland Park 44 —
The Marine National Park 44 — Wats 45 —
Other places to visit 46

10 Things to do 48
Meditation 48 — Museums 49 — Cycling 50 —
Diving 51 — Thai boxing 52 — Buffalo fighting 54 —
Cockfighting 55 — Fishing 55 — Snooker 56 —
Massage 56

11 Island hopping excursions 58
Koh Phangan 58 — Koh Tao 59

12 General information 61
Drugs 61 — Health 61 — Sunburn 63 — Taking the
children 63 — Cheating 63 — Time difference 64 —
Renewing visas 64 — Tax 65

Appendix 1
Accommodation listings 67

Appendix 2
Useful addresses 79

Appendix 3
Useful words and phrases 81

Index 83

ONE

Introducing Koh Samui

In the two years we spent on the beautiful, tropical island of Koh Samui, we met only one *farang* (Thai for foreigner) who was not happy with the place. This was a Californian fellow who complained that it was not at all like Venice beach near Los Angeles. This is true; anyone expecting muscle-bound posers, roller skaters or street artists will find these in short supply.

However, Koh Samui does have a wealth of attractions. From peace and tranquillity to wild parties, there is a healthy cross-section to suit most moods and tastes.

Have you ever seen one of those TV ads showing beautiful and voluptuous young things discovering Paradise on some remote, tropical spot? Well, Koh Samui is it! In fact, we have witnessed this sort of advertisement being filmed here.

Not so long ago, Samui was a back-packers retreat. Anyone worn out by travelling through India or trekking in Nepal would take the boat and chug slowly to this remote spot. At that time, there was no electricity, no running water and very little accommodation. In the mid-seventies travellers were still camping on the beach or living with friendly local Samuians for very little monetary outlay.

But the breathtaking beauty of this island could not be kept a secret for too long and, as the average traveller became more adventurous, so the island began slowly to be visited by more people. Within the space of just ten years, Koh Samui has been transformed, and the main economy of the island now is tourism, as opposed to the coconut and the fishing trades of previous years. Nowadays, there is no

KOH SAMUI

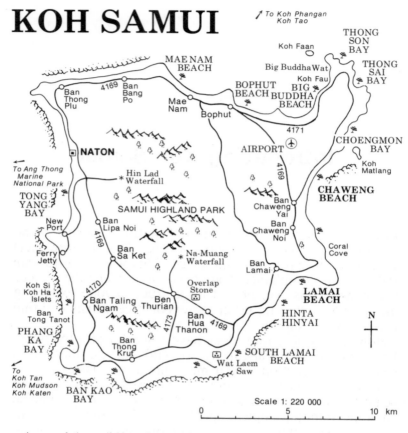

To Koh Phangan
Koh Tao

THONG SON BAY

Koh Faan

Big Buddha Wat
Koh Fau

THONG SAI BAY

MAE NAM BEACH

BOPHUT BEACH
BIG BUDDHA BEACH

Ban Thong Plu

4169 Ban Bang Po

Mae Nam

Bophut

4171

NATON

AIRPORT

CHOENGMON BAY

Koh Matlang

To Ang Thong Marine National Park

Hin Lad Waterfall

4169

CHAWENG BEACH

TONG YANG BAY

SAMUI HIGHLAND PARK

Ban Chaweng Yai

New Port

Ban Lipa Noi

Ban Chaweng Noi

Coral Cove

4169

Ferry Jetty

Ban Sa Ket

Na-Muang Waterfall

Ban Lamai

Koh Si Koh Ha Islets

4170

Overlap Stone

LAMAI BEACH

Ban Tong Tanot

Ban Taling Ngam

Ben Thurian

4173

Ban Hua Thanon

4169

HINTA HINYAI

N

PHANG KA BAY

Ban Thong Krut

SOUTH LAMAI BEACH

To Koh Tan Koh Mudson Koh Katen

Wat Laem Saw

BAN KAO BAY

Scale 1: 220 000

0   5   10 km

Accommodation available at the two most popular beaches, listed from north to south :-

☆ CHAWENG BEACH

Samui I.	Lotus	Magic Light	Chaweng G.H.
Matlang	Sun East	Liberty	Seaside
Blue Lagoon	Coconut Gro.	Riviara	First
Venus	Samui Pk.	Royal Inn	Fair
Marine	Coral Pk.	Viking	Chaweng Pal.
Moon	Chaweng Gdn.	Thai Ho.	Mellow
Family	J.R.	Village	New Star
K. John	Best Beach	Pansea	Imperial Samui
O.P.	Chaweng Top	Wisan	Sunshine
Samui Cabana	Malibu	Arabian	Relax
The Island	Long	Chaweng Cabana	Maeo
Chaweng	Thai	Joy	Tawee
Monthin	King Star	Munchies	Chaweng Noi
Lucky Mother	Chaba Samui	White Ho.	Tropicana

☆ LAMAI BEACH

Marine	Coconut V.	Sea Breeze	P.N.
Wish	Weekender	Golden Sand	White Sand
Lamai	Coconut B.	Aloha	Chain
Sand Sea	Lamai Inn	Vineyard Haven	Nice
Garden Home	Animal Ho.	Casanovas	Palm
The Pavilion	Best	Lamai Pearl	Sunrise
Mui	Thai Ho. Inn	Bill	Hin Yai
Fantasy	Marina	Paradise	Hin Ta
Magic	Mira Mare	Green Canyon	Anika

problem with regular running water or electricity, and the coming of the airport in April 1989 was, in the eyes of many people, a great improvement. Accommodation can be found from as little as 50 baht a night for basic huts on the beach, and up to US$200 a night for a luxury hotel room. But do not panic! Despite all the modern "improvements", Koh Samui still manages to retain a quality of timelessness and has not yet become just another overcrowded holiday resort with all the usual tourist traps. But please note: we would like to point out that obviously places affected by the tourist trade undergo change; therefore the reader may find some minor alterations have occurred since the writing of this book.

Location and physical features

Lying some 700 kilometres south of Bangkok in the Gulf of Thailand is the island of Koh Samui (*Koh* means island). Its native inhabitants call themselves *Chao Samuians*, which means "people of Samui". The main island covers some 280 square kilometres of gentle hills and pristine white-sand beaches lined with picturesque coconut plantations and lapped by clear water. It is surrounded by eighty smaller islands, six of which — Pangan, Ta Loy, Tao, Tan, Mah Koh and Ta Pao — are also inhabited and all within a boat ride of Koh Samui.

Because of the island's hill-like structure and thick concentration of trees, the population is concentrated around its edges, the main town being Naton (it rhymes with baton) on the west side, facing the mainland. Naton is a port and fishing town, and houses three banks, a post office, a small daily food market, three supermarkets, and an abundance of clothes shops and bars. An excellent, wide concrete road, Highway 4169, encircles the island, with occasional roads and unpaved dirt tracks linking the beaches and villages with remote bungalows. Distance markers are shown in kilometres, and their frequency makes it hard to get lost on the island.

Seasons: when to go

Samui, being an island, is naturally exposed; weatherwise, most Westerners prefer to visit between February and May but, generally, Samui boasts a warm and temperate climate all the year round. Rain may or may not fall in the rainy or monsoon season and may be accompanied by magnificent electrical storms, brightening up the evening skies in short successive bursts, presenting the black tempestuous seas in spectacular flashes. Even the locals never really seem to know what may occur weatherwise but, in theory, there are three distinct seasons:

- **February to May** is ideal for most Westerners, with temperatures around eighty to eighty-five degrees Fahrenheit, clear blue skies and a fresh breeze. The evenings are slightly cooler.
- **June to September** has temperatures of well over ninety degrees, and can sometimes be pretty humid. This is also the monsoon time, and there may be heavy rains, which, we found, seem to occur either in the morning, clearing up for the afternoon, or vice versa.
- **October to January** is hot, with occasional heavy rain.

What to take

Travel as light as possible; take lightweight cotton shorts, T-shirts and dresses, and maybe casual wear for the evenings or for such things as visiting Wats (women are not permitted to enter wearing shorts!). As it is mostly rather warm, light clothing is best, and sandals and thongs are ideal and generally sufficient as casual footwear. Clothes and footwear can be purchased cheaply in Naton should the need arise. Sunglasses, toiletries and accessories too can be bought for little cost.

Shorts, sarongs and T-shirts are the normal mode of dress, both for day and evening wear. Being overdressed can look slightly ridiculous out there, although this trend is slowly changing as more and more of the designer clothes brigade arrive from Europe.

It would be a good idea to take a practical first-aid kit,

comprising disinfectant cream, band-aids and dressings. These items can be purchased easily on the island, but we have found that the cream and powder treatments sold are pretty well ineffective.

Documentation

All non-Thais require a full passport to enter Thailand. There are three types of visa: transit, non-immigrant tourist and immigrant. The former two are applicable if you are to visit Thailand as a tourist.

The best idea is to obtain a 30 or 60 day (depending on your proposed length of stay) non-immigrant tourist visa from the Thai embassy or consulate in your own country before leaving. This costs around £12.00 or US$20 plus 3 photographs. However, the costs do vary depending on your nationality. Swedes for instance pay nothing. This visa allows you to enter Thailand within three months of the date of issue. You can also apply for this visa in a neigh-bouring country to Thailand if you are travelling around for some months before entering Thailand. The address of the Thai embassy in England is 30 Queens Gate, London SW7 5SB. Tel 071-589 0173.

The non-immigrant tourist visa can be renewed once in Thailand. Please see Renewing Visas in Chapter 12.

If you do not obtain the visa before entering Thailand you can obtain a 15 day transit visa upon entry to the country at a cost of around US$5. When the 15 day visa expires you have to leave the country to obtain a non-immigrant tourist visa (as explained above and in Chapter 12) from a neighbouring country to allow you to re-enter and stay.

Money

The Thai unit of currency is the baht (100 satang). As with any currency, the exchange rate of the baht fluctuates although it is not as erratic as many other Asian currencies. The rate for the last two years has hovered around the following levels: US dollar equals about 25 baht; Australian dollar equals about 22 baht; pound sterling equals about 40 baht.

Denominations and colours of notes are: 10 baht (brown), 20 baht (green), 50 baht (blue), 100 baht (red), 500 baht (purple). The 20, 50 and sometimes even the 500 baht notes can look similar and may be easily confused when they are old or crumpled.

The coins in most common usage are 1 and 5 baht, and people unused to the money are warned of the similarity in size between these. The 1 baht is a nickel-and-silver coin; 2 and 5 baht coins are copper edged. Smaller denomination satang, made of brass, are in circulation, but are virtually worthless to a *farang*, and one of these coins would not purchase a peanut. Currency exchange booths are springing up all around the island, and good rates of exchange are normally offered at these and the banks, with travellers cheques usually getting a better rate than cash.

Credit cards such as American Express, Visa and Access are normally accepted only at the larger hotels and at banks, so should not be relied upon as the main method of payment in most transactions.

The Thai Farmers and the Siam City Banks, on the 4169, are the two main banks of Naton, business hours being 9am-3.30pm. If a currency note is dropped, it should not be stood upon, as the Thai will find this a great insult. The King is held in the highest esteem; the feet are considered to be the unholiest part of the body, being the nearest to the ground, just as the head is considered to be the holiest. To place a foot upon a picture of the monarch is unthinkable to the Thai.

One last point of interest about money: tipping is not common practice on Koh Samui, and in fact some Thais will not understand what is happening when someone tries to tip them.

TWO

How to get there

Your journey to Samui will be in stages, and the number of stages will of course depend on where you are setting out from and the route you take. There are two mainland departure points for the island: **Bangkok**, from where you can get direct flights to Koh Samui; and **Surat Thani**, the provincial capital, from where there is a ferry service.

From Bangkok: direct

Bangkok Airways offers six daily direct flights from Bangkok to Koh Samui, with a seventh flight Monday to Thursday. The fare is 1650 baht for a one-way journey of one hour and ten minutes in their twin engine turbo prop aircraft. Flight times are: 7.30, 8.00, 10.40, 13.20, 13.50, 16.30 and 17.00. Return flights times are: 9.00, 11.40, 12.10, 14.50, 15.20, 18.00 and 18.30.

Getting to Bangkok
Bangkok lies on a popular worldwide route, and can be reached easily and not too expensively from most western countries. For travellers in Asia the following approximate single, tourist class price guide may be useful: to Bangkok from Singapore US$140; Hong-Kong US$190; Kuala Lumpur US$120; Taipei US$250; Calcutta US$140; Kathmandu US$200; Colombo US$220; New Delhi US$190; Manila US$250.

The airport at Koh Samui

For those arriving by plane, the sight of Samui looming into view is quite spectacular. The recently constructed airport, small in size, as might be expected, is situated amongst the coconut trees close to Big Buddha. There is a bar for those in need of refreshment, but generally most people pass quickly through the airport to the many waiting buses and taxis. Coaches wait to pick up package tours, and private bungalow owners offer accommodation. The taxis, which are basically small covered trucks, display their destination just above the driver's seat. Twenty baht should be the absolute maximum fare for a ride from the airport, although many drivers will try to get more.

Passing through the airport is quick and easy; there is nowhere on the island which lies further than a ride of three-quarters of an hour from the airport, and so most people can be on the beach within an hour of arriving by plane.

From Surat Thani: by ferry

Songsern Travel operates the express boat service from Ban Don (the ferry boarding point at Surat Thani) three times daily. Train and coach passengers are transported from Surat Thani to the boat in a 15-minute coach ride. The crossing from Ban Don to Koh Samui takes two hours, and costs 90 baht one way, 165 baht return fare. There is also a night boat, which takes five hours, on which passengers can sleep over. Boats leave Surat Thani at 7.30, 12.00 and 14.00. Returning boats leave Koh Samui at 7.30, 12.00 and 15.00.

Three daily car ferries also depart from Don Sak pier, which is 60 kilometres or one hour away from Surat Thani. The crossing to Koh Samui takes one hour 15 minutes. Buses from Surat Thani to Don Sak charge a 10 baht fare and leave at 9.00, 14.00 and 17.30. Fares for the ferry are 180 baht for a car with driver, 40 baht for a pedestrian and 70 baht for a motorbike and rider.

Getting to Surat Thani

● **By air**
Thai International Airways has two regular daily flights from Bangkok to Surat Thani, at 11.00 and 18.50, increasing to three a day in peak season, the fare being about 1445 baht. For a further 150 baht, the airline also offers a limousine/boat service from the airport to Koh Samui via the express boat from Ban Don. Should direct flights to Samui be fully booked then the more hurried traveller may wish to fly to the provincial capital of Surat Thani and from there take the ferry to the island. The alternative to flying is by road or rail to Surat Thani and again from there by ferry from either Don Sak or Ban Don piers.

● **By rail**
Two daily departures from Hua Lampong, the main railway station in Bangkok, take you on the twelve-hour overnight journey to Surat Thani for about 125 baht for third-class seating, 244 baht for second-class seating, 314 baht for a second-class upper berth sleeper, 344 baht for a second-class lower berth sleeper, and 424 baht for a second-class air-conditioned sleeper.
Trains depart Bangkok at 17.30, 18.30 and 19.20, arriving at Surat Thani at 4.59, 6.30 and 6.34 respectively. The boat for Koh Samui leaves at 7.30 and there are buses immediately outside the railway station at Surat Thani to take you to the ferry boarding pier.
For the return journey, boats leave Koh Samui at 12.00 noon and 15.00, to connect with trains departing Surat Thani at 17.35, 18.20, 18.54, 19.23 and 20.12, arriving at Bangkok at 5.10, 5.50, 6.10, 6.35 and 7.05.

● **By coach or bus**
The Southern Bus Terminal on Charan Sanitwong Road, near the railway station in Bangkok, is the departure point for buses to Surat Thani, where all buses and trains stop en route to Koh Samui.
One bus leaves in the morning, and there is also an overnight bus for the ten to twelve hours trip, costing 225 baht on a non-air-conditioned bus, and 320 baht on an air-conditioned one. They are generally comfortable enough

to grab some sleep along the way but, if taking an air-conditioned vehicle, please ensure you have plenty of clothes to put on, as the air-conditioning tends to make the journey pretty cold, and usually only one thin blanket is provided.

Unfortunately, thefts are fairly common on the night bus, so take care of your belongings.

Many travel agents can be found along Khao San Road in Bangkok, a street well known for offering cheap accommodation, flights and restaurants for the budget traveller. Here, a quick and easy booking may be made for seats on the bus from Bangkok to Koh Samui, all inclusive for about 350 baht with one of the private operators.

Surat Thani can also be reached by five-hour journeys in air-conditioned mini-buses from Phuket and Hat Yai. The 220 baht fare includes the boat trip to Koh Samui.

For the return journey from Koh Samui to Bangkok, there are two air-conditioned buses which leave from near the ferry pier in Naton daily at 13.30 and 15.30, arriving in Bangkok at 5.00, with a short stop in Surat Thani. Bookings can be arranged through any of the numerous travel agents in Naton, although we found those on the same road as the pier to be the most reliable in our own experience, but please check all details thoroughly before travelling.

THREE

The island and its people

Historical background

The history of Koh Samui as an inhabited island goes back fifteen hundred years. The first people to arrive and live there were fishermen, seeking shelter from the winds in the protected waters of Mae Nam Bay and Bo Phut Bay, which are now popular and still relatively peaceful beaches on the north shore of the island. These settlers found the waters around the island very rich in many varieties of seafood, and on the island itself the soil was also extremely fertile, making it the ideal place for small communities of people to establish and cultivate a lifestyle for themselves.

Koh Samui's character as an island of cosy fishing villages remained the same throughout many centuries, until the late 1970s when budget travellers discovered it as a resting place on their travels throughout Asia. By 1980 it was also a main destination of the backpacker, owing to its stunning paradisiacal beauty and the then extremely cheap food and basic accommodation.

Since then, Koh Samui has become increasingly popular; but it still remained essentially an island more specifically for the traveller on a shoestring budget until even as recently as April 1989, when the small airport was opened which now brings in six or seven flights a day from Bangkok. This boost to the tourist industry is, inevitably, changing the personality of the island and obviously brings with it both advantages and disadvantages, depending on whether you are a tourist on holiday for just two weeks, or a traveller staying for two months. The real appeal of the island is its ability to cater for a great variety of lifestyles, but now is the time to go there, before tourism gets the chance to completely engulf this paradise.

Whether you choose to go independently or book through a travel agent, whether you opt for the quiet life, spending next to nothing, or live the high life, spending a fortune, there is no doubt that you will want to return to Koh Samui. This happens to all its visitors — it happened to us, and we stayed for two years!

The people

Generally, today, the Thai person is a cultural mix of Yunans from China, the Shars of northern Burma and the Mons and Laotians from the north and from the east of Khmer. However, the Thai people who live on Koh Samui regard themselves as different because they are islanders and obviously do lead a different lifestyle from the rest of Thailand.

Their main source of income is from the tourist industry, as well as the coconut and fishing industries. The majority of people live in an extended family situation and have a small area of land to grow vegetables and fruit, and maybe keep a few chickens and pigs, which allows them to be mostly self-sufficient. Alternatively, they may keep bungalows, cafés and bars on the beaches.

In general, they have a very laid-back lifestyle. Entertainment for women seems to be eating and gossiping, whilst the men go to bullfights and cockfights.

Religion

The majority of Samuians claim to be believers of **Buddhism** of the Theravada type (lesser vehicle).

The Buddhist brotherhood, the Sangha, is visible all over Samui, and you will see the orange-robed monks at the Wats and also sometimes in the early morning, wandering heads down, with their food bowls. Most young males are expected to spend some of their youth leading the monastic life; this is usually between leaving school and marrying, though not always. Three months is normally the length of time they stay in the Wat (monastery), and this period starts in July.

Mahanikai and Thammayut are the two sects of the Sangha. The latter monks usually lead a more regimented life; they must reach a high standard of meditation and obtain a scholarship of Buddhism. The days of the monks are usually spent in meditation, chanting the Dhamma, taking care of the Wat and walking with their alms bowls in the mornings to obtain their daily ration of food.

There are four noble truths and the eight-fold path which form the basis of the Buddhist philosophy (see box).

The Four Noble Truths

1. The truth of suffering — "Existence is suffering."
2. The truth of the cause of suffering — "Suffering is caused by desire."
3. The truth of the cessation of suffering — "Eliminate the cause of suffering (desire) and suffering will cease to arise."
4. The truth of the path — "The eight fold path is the way to eliminate desire/extinguish suffering."

The Eight-Fold Path

1. Right understanding
2. Right mindedness
3. Right speech
4. Right bodily conduct
5. Right livelihood
6. Right effort
7. Right attentiveness
8. Right concentration

We found that the locals have added to the basic doctrines a superstitious belief in spirits and demons. On the whole, though, most islanders do not seem to practise their religion to any great degree; the idea of compassion to all creatures is certainly not adhered to in general, cockfights and bullfights being very popular, and Western visitors should be prepared for the sight of injured animals left to suffer without any human aid, since to cease suffering in this life means the being must suffer again in the next.

There is also a minority **Muslim** group, made up mostly of the poorer fishermen and their families, whilst many of the wealthier families have become **Christians** and there are a number of Catholic schools and churches around the island. Whether there is a connection between money and choice of religion is for the individual to decide.

Customs

Visitors must always remove their shoes before entering a temple or holy place, and clothing such as shorts or revealing blouses should definitely be avoided.

Women must never touch or sit beside a monk; Buddha considered himself to be so handsome and sexually appealing that women became his biggest distraction when following the eight-fold path, and therefore any intimacy with women was banned. It is considered insulting for a woman to attempt any communication with a monk, including directly handing him anything, although it is all right to do so through a third party.

Lovers please note: kissing or embracing intimately in public is a definite no-no, but we would comment that this is one custom that seems to have fallen by the wayside on Koh Samui!

Saving face is all important to a Thai, and loss of temper or impatience in the face of what may seem a ridiculous situation to a Westerner will do no good at all. We ourselves had many examples of what seemed to be sheer stubbornness, perhaps the most ludicrous being when we tried to buy a local bus ticket from Haadyai to Surat Thani. The young girl behind the counter told us that the 4pm bus we wanted (and had taken before) did not exist, and had never run at that time. We went to another counter, where the male assistant confirmed that there was indeed a 4pm bus but told us that we had to buy our ticket from the girl. On returning to her counter, rather than admit to a mistake and thus lose face, the girl refused to sell us a ticket. We ended up taking the train instead that day.

Officially, no image of Buddha is allowed to be taken out of the country, because of the belief that it will not be treated with adequate respect in another country not of the Buddhist faith. However, visitors wishing to take home such a memento may apply for a permit at the Fine Arts department of the National Museum, situated near the Grand Palace in Bangkok.

Festivals

We were sorry to observe that Samuians were not the most festive-minded people to be encountered in South East Asia — far from it, in fact. The only exception to this is the Songkran Festival from 13 to 15 April, this being the New Year's celebrations of the lunar year in Thailand, which can be witnessed in the main town of Naton.

Buddha images are bathed. Monks and elders receive the respect of younger Thais by sprinkling water over their hands. This can, and does, develop into a free-for-all, with buckets of water being tossed about in all directions. We have heard that, at this time of year, one can even throw water over the policemen and get away with it, although we never put this to the test!

For the rest of the year, tourists will not generally encounter too much local celebration except that on the beaches the Christian Christmas is celebrated, also New Year's Eve, owing to the fact that the majority of the population are tourists/travellers and Western.

FOUR

Transport

Taxis

Taxis, or *songthaews* as they are called, form the main means of transport around the island. They are small, narrow, covered van-type vehicles, designed to seat about a dozen, but the drivers will load on as many passengers as possible. Service is quite good, running frequently between towns and beaches.

Official maximum fares are set but, as stated previously, drivers frequently try to charge more, and the traveller must be firm whenever possible. Examples of official fares from Naton are:

- to Mae Nam, Bo Phut or Thaling Ngam: 15 baht;
- to Big Buddha, Chaweng, Lamai, or Thong Grud: 20 baht;
- to Choeng Mon: 20 baht.

A night taxi service runs between Chaweng and Lamai every hour, and costs 20 baht. Evening taxis also run from some of the quieter beaches to the Reggae Pub in Chaweng. Timetables can be found all over the place, but local bungalow owners can sometimes arrange a pick-up if the group for the service is large enough.

Vehicle hire

Motor bikes can be hired almost anywhere, with small 85cc models costing around 150 baht for a day. Half-day hire for about 80 to 100 baht can sometimes be arranged, but is not encouraged unless business is slack. The 125cc trek bikes cost from 200 baht per day, and larger bikes can be hired in Naton from 300 baht, although these latter charges have been rising lately.

We found the 85cc bikes to be the least troublesome, although road-handling is not as good on these as on the larger models. The main problem with the 125cc bike is that it does not have a petrol gauge, which means that the rider frequently runs out of fuel, dirt gets sucked into the carburettor, and, after a few such incidents, the bike will cease to operate after warming up. Everything seems fine until the rider is a few miles along on his trip, when the bike suddenly stops, and the only thing to do then is to be patient and wait for the machine to cool down.

All bikes should be thoroughly checked before being taken out, as many of them are definitely sub-standard, with bad brakes, bald tyres and missing wing mirrors often being the norm. Jeeps can also be hired all over the island from about 500 baht a day, but these are often in an appalling condition, with brakes that pull to one side (when they actually work at all) and steering which can be ridiculously slack. Some of the larger car companies charge about 1000 baht a day for jeep hire, but at least their vehicles are normally roadworthy. As with the bikes, all vehicles should be carefully checked before taking out for hire — one emergency stop we made found the car careering towards the edge of a steep drop after the driver's side brake jammed suddenly. We were lucky, others are not.

Please note that exceptional care is advised when riding or driving along as, unfortunately, road accidents and deaths are extremely common in Samui, the main causes being a combination of drunk or stoned drivers, substandard vehicles and disgraceful road conditions. Bandaged road accident victims form an all too common sight and in August 1989, eight tourists were killed in one week. We personally avoided any driving at night.

Insurance can be taken out, but most hirers are indifferent to whether or not this is done, as the *farang* normally pays, no matter whose fault an accident may be. Nine times out of ten, the stranger on the Samuians' territory will be the one to foot the bill. Although it is not a common practice, the police also have the right to stop drivers, and those not carrying their licences may be fined. It is as well to be forewarned.

Petrol stations

There is no shortage of petrol stations on the island. For those with motor bikes, there are services at frequent intervals. These consist of a simple oil drum with a measuring device and pump fitted to the top. A litre of petrol is 10 baht.

FIVE

Accommodation

A comprehensive list of accommodation available in Koh Samui appears in Appendix 1. This section describes in general what to expect for your money.

Bungalows

Most of Samui's accommodation is of the bungalow type, although the word bungalow may be misleading to many Westerners, for whom it may conjure up a picture of a small house, which is not the case here. Most of Samui's bungalows are made of wood, covered with thatched roofs.

In the cheaper accommodations, washing facilities are communal (which means that women use the same facilities as men but not necessarily at the same time), and can mean having a wash from a large earthenware jug, with a pot for throwing water over oneself. Actually, this is not too much of a hardship, especially for seasoned travellers, bearing in mind that the temperature is usually pretty warm all year round. Cockroach and insect haters, however, might be advised to avoid this sort of dwelling.

A lot of toilets are the squat type, or "ski jump" as we once heard them described.

• Basic bungalow accommodation is usually one room comprising a bed, sheets and sometimes a mosquito net. They start from about 50 baht and this is per bungalow per night to sleep two people, excluding meals. There is always a café or restaurant attached to the bungalows serving Thai and Western type food and numerous ones to choose from

25

nearby so eating is not a problem.

● For between 80-100 baht a fan is usually included.

● From about 100-150 baht bungalows normally have a double bed, mosquito net, fan and adjoining shower and toilet.

● Around 150-250 baht will usually get you a bigger, cleaner and newer bungalow.

● From 250 up to 600 baht most bungalows have modern showers and toilets, and even wardrobes and seating.

● Above 600 baht brick bungalows with air conditioning are available.

Self-catering accommodation

This is extremely rare; those requiring it must look out for advertisements for houses. This can, however, be quite a cheap way of living for anyone planning to stay for more than a month.

Hotels

There are a few hotels, with some of the higher priced ones being typical of hotels all around the world, with the usual amenities.

SIX

Food and drink

The Thai diet

The basis of a Thai meal is rice, normally steamed, and on Koh Samui mainly white; the local people, in fact, serve it with practically every meal. This could explain why many long-term visitors to the island (and men more than women, for some reason) lose a fair bit of weight.

Rice is similar to most cereals in so much as it is predominantly made up of carbohydrate which provides us with energy. It is however relatively low in protein — about six to seven percent — and contains only the B-Group vitamins plus minerals such as calcium and iron. It is therefore an extremely good staple food but must be part of a varied balanced diet.

Luckily, the Thais use an abundance of fresh vegetables, fish and meat to provide the necessary balance. Vegetables are often less than a day old, and fish may literally have been swimming around a mere matter of hours before arriving, beautifully cooked, on the plate.

Thais prefer hot, spicy dishes, so those with delicate palates should approach some of the curries with caution, although we must emphasise that ninety-nine percent of the time the *farang* will be eating Thai dishes greatly adapted to Western taste. Most Samuians are surprised when faced with a Westerner who wants to eat as the locals do.

Chillis are added in almost explosive quantities to hot dishes — beware of the small red or green torpedo-like variety, called Prik Kee-Noo locally! The Thais also have their own hot, extra hot or even hotter sauces, which may be added quite liberally, so be sure to specify your preference emphatically. If the food is too hot for your taste, eat plenty of rice; do not try to reduce any burning sensation with cooling drinks, which may give momentary relief, but which actually intensify the effect. Coconut curries are marvellous, and can be ordered with or without chilli.

Some Thai delicacies

Tom yam is Thailand's contribution to the culinary arts; it is a sour soup which can be made with various meats or fish, the most famous version being made with prawns (*tom yam goong*). The basic broth is flavoured with lemon grass, citrus leaves, lime juice, fish sauce and hot chillis.
Gaeng liang fak thong: pumpkin and coconut.
Gaeng chud: consommé with stuffed mushrooms.
Gai tom kah: chicken cooked in coconut milk.
Gaeng kalee goong: lobster and prawn curry.
Pad preo wan goong: sweet and sour shrimps.
Poo cha: stuffed crab shells.
Hoh mok hoy: steamed mussels.
Pla mueg pad prik: fried squid with hot sauce.
Pla khao lad prik: fried garoupa with chilli sauce.
Pla pad king: sea bass with fresh ginger.
Gaeng kua nuer: fish and vegetable curry.
Pla kaha is a ten-foot carp, and is an inhabitant of the rivers of Thailand.
Gai obb bai toey: fried chicken in pandan leaves.
Gaeng phed: duck and vegetables.
Gaeng phed gat: curried chicken.
Tom kem gai: chicken casserole (Note: chicken, although fresh, is generally pretty scrawny and less tasty than its Western counterpart, probably because it is naturally bred.)
Khao obb sapparod: fried rice in pineapple.
Khao pad prik: fried curried rice.
Khao soi: curried noodles.
Kaeb moo: crispy fried pork (*moo* is nothing to do with a cow!).
Gaeng kiew wan: green beef curry.
Yam neau: Thai beef salad.

Pad luke chin: steamed pork balls with vegetables.
Pad kow-port onn gab gai: baby corn with chicken.
Pak tom ka-ti: vegetables boiled in coconut milk.
Pak dong: pickled vegetables.

Fruit

Exotic, tropical fruits can be found, and full advantage should be taken of the varieties that grow on Koh Samui. Some of the less familiar ones are:

Mango: can be eaten when still green or when ripe. *Kao neo mamuang* is mango with sticky rice, a popular Thai dessert.

Durian: the smell from this fruit is undeniably pungent, and can be a bit off-putting. It has a hard, greenish-yellow-brown shell with sharp thorns, but its flesh is juicy and sweet. Well worth a try.

Rambutan: about the size of a plum, it is oval in shape, red/green in colour and has a sort of long bristled skin. The flesh is white and could be compared to the lychee in flavour.

Jackfruit: a large fruit, encased by a thick skin and soft thorns, it has a yellow, tangy flesh.

Mangosteen: recognisable by its thick, dark purple skin, the pulp is in segments, and has a sweet juicy flavour.

A handful of restaurants

Most restaurants in Koh Samui have plenty of Western dishes on the menu and there is, in fact, a great variety of specialised restaurants, such as Chinese, Italian, Swiss, etc. Here are a few which we found to be particularly good, basing our judgement on quality of food, value and service.

General

Bird in Hand Bo Phut. One of our favourite places. The menu is on the wall, and Western-style food is cooked here. The proprietor is an Englishman who likes a good chat, and who will do everything he can to ensure your meal is to your liking. He gives great value for money, and this is a good place for breakfast, dinner and your evening meal; the home-made bread is terrific.

Madam Sim on the Chaweng beach road facing Lucky Mothers. One of the few eating places open late. Closing at 11pm, it takes the last orders at 10pm, and fresh fish can be ordered from an outside display.

Suneast Bungalow on Chaweng Beach. An excellent place to eat Thai or Western food, both very well cooked at good prices, and served in pleasant surroundings.

For those of you wanting late night snacks, there is an excellent little stall open until the small hours, serving Thai food only. It is off the Chaweng beach road, on the Chicago Disco turn-off, by the Rock Pub.

Lamai's main resort area abounds with various restaurants, but unfortunately many of them lack consistency in quality of food and service, possible due to the quick turnover of management. Most palates can be satisfied here, but it is generally a matter of trial and error to find a good meal.

Chinese

Phallung Restaurant situated on the 4169 route, just on the corner of the Na Muang Waterfall turn-off. It is set on a pretty little site, with a tiny artificial waterfall adding to its splendour. There is an excellent and extensive choice of both Chinese and Western food, at very reasonable prices.

Lotus Restaurant on the Chaweng beach road, between the Green Mango and the Black Cat in a small shopping parade. The setting may put some people off, but once the very well-priced food is sampled, they return again and again. Try the duck dishes; the beer here is also very cheap.

The Wisan is actually on the beach in a very pleasant setting; it has a large bar and good sound system and shows nightly videos.

Fiesta Night Club on the opposite side of the road, is probably the most prominent spot in the area.

OP Bungalows on Chaweng Beach do a very good Chinese meal.

Italian

Italian food can be found all around the island, especially if pizzas are what you are after.

The Fountain Naton. We found this to be the best one. It is halfway up Middle Road, and it is run by an Italian couple.

Swiss

There are a number of Swiss restaurants, most of them slightly dearer than average.

Swiss Chalet on the 4169 route at Lamai has the best food. It is very good for group bookings; food is served in generous quantities, and specialities can be ordered in advance. They also have a large garden for diners who prefer to eat in the open air.

Swedish

The Vastervik to the south of Naton, at Taling Ngam Beach. Highly recommended. It is run by a Thai who spent a long time in Sweden, and its only disadvantage is that it is difficult to reach without transport. Follow the 4170 road until reaching a large gate on the right — you cannot miss it as there are also two life-size statues of elephants — and keep to that road until you see the Taling Ngam turn-off. Good dormitories are available from as little as fifty baht and really nice bungalows from two hundred baht, so why not plan on making a night of it? Wine, dine and chat to your heart's content, watch the fabulous sunset and relax completely, knowing that your bed is not far away.

Indian

The Mariam just off the 4169, on the road to the main Lamai beach, one of the first buildings in the first group of shops on the right. A Muslim restaurant specialising in Indian dishes, it is well worth a visit. Its very basic decor makes it look just like a working man's café, but the food is good.

Seafood

Fish is bought fresh every day from the market in Naton, and seafood dishes are therefore available in abundance all over the island.

Eden Seafood Restaurant at the top end of Chaweng beach road is one of our favourite places. Although dearer than most restaurants, its beautiful setting on a lake, its wide selection of fish dishes, always fresh and excellently cooked, make it a place not to be missed.

Drinks

The local brews are Singha beer, Kloster beer, Mekong whisky and Hong Yok whisky.

Both beers are not too bad but they are of the lager type which must be consumed cold. Singha contains a preservative commonly used in embalming fluid and this can leave an odd taste in the mouth, but there is an alternative available called Singha Gold, which is a lighter, less alcoholic beer. Recognisable by the lion-type symbol on the labels, Singha and Singha Gold cost about 35-40 baht. Kloster beer is somewhat smoother to drink and costs 40-45 baht.

Mekong whisky is notorious for its effect. We have seen people who are regular drinkers of this brew change character over a period of time. It is thicker, sweeter and far easier to drink than the conventional whiskies, and its price of only 65-70 baht a half-bottle makes it a popular choice with budget travellers. Also, because it is lower in alcohol content than our whisky, some people are encouraged to drink far more.

We ran a couple of bars on the island for some time, and a familiar comment from new samplers of Mekong whisky was, "This stuff isn't doing anything for me," only to be followed the next day by, "What the hell happened last night?" So be warned! This drink is a definite "creeper", and most people prefer to mix it with Coke and ice. Some bars do a type of package deal consisting of a half-bottle of Mekong, a bucket of ice and enough Coke for a good mix for about 110 baht.

Hong Yok whisky is a rougher and slightly cheaper version of Mekong, at about 60-65 baht. A lot of places will try to palm it off as genuine Mekong so be on guard; Hong Yok has a yellow label, whilst the Mekong label is almost orange.

European and Australian beers can also be purchased in supermarkets and bars. The former charge about 45-50 baht against the 55-65 baht charged by the latter.

All the usual spirits are available on the island and are quite reasonable in relation to Western prices. Australian and some European wines can be found in most supermarkets and many bars, but they are often quite bruised after bumpy transportation. Often the wines are kept in the intense heat, which can ruin them. For these reasons, a cheap wine can sometimes be more palatable than a dearer one, but it is really a matter of pot luck.

Bars

The island is loaded with bars of all shapes and sizes, many of them being what may be called "Girlie" bars, managed by *farangs* who employ prostitutes to work them. Lamai and Chaweng are full of such places, most of them pumping out loud music, with passing men being hailed by the "ladies of the night" with, "Where you go, sexy man?" There is not a great deal to choose between them, but different nationals may head for those bars displaying the flag of their own country.

Dave's GB Bar, on the Chaweng beach road, opposite the Black Cat complex, is a bar with a little more character. There is a dart board, a small dancing spot and nice seating arrangements. Dave and his partner Kevin are extremely hospitable, and it is a good place to go if you want to find out what is happening on the island.

The Reggae Pub is the busiest place on Koh Samui (some say the busiest in Thailand). Situated in a complex of bars and small eating establishments off the Chaweng beach road, it is extensively sign-posted and can be recognised by a large sign showing the head of Bob Marley. Despite the name, reggae is rarely played here; the music is mainly repetitive pop music, and a sandpit is provided for dancing. A large circular bar ensures fairly quick service. Most people head for this bar after midnight, and sunrise finds the place still open. The one exception to the "after midnight" norm is Sunday evening, when beer drinking contests are held. This place is an all-nighter with plenty of drinking, dancing and general merriment, and food stalls surround it for people with the late night appetite.

The Island is a great bar at the north end of Chaweng, and one of the few to be found on the beach. It is, in fact, a group of bungalows with a large circular bar in a tropical setting looking straight out to sea. People who want to get away from the madding crowd would do well to make for this place; the music is good, cocktails are reasonably priced, and they serve Western and Thai food of exceptional quality. The bar opens at 6pm and closes when the last customer leaves; the restaurant is open all day, with last orders taken about 9pm. The proprietor is an American gentleman and a great host, and service is very efficient here by Thai standards. Look out for the parties which are quite a regular feature of the place and extremely good fun.

Flamingo is more of a discotheque than a bar. It is situated in the main Lamai complex, and is probably the most popular place in Lamai, with the usual repetitive pop music and disco feel to it — a late night spot. Thai boxing tournaments and various shows are occasionally held here.

The Chicago in Chaweng is run by the same people as the Flamingo, and is an almost exact copy, but this one to date is frequented mostly by the local Thais.

The Green Mango has an open air wood and thatched roof layout and is situated on the road which runs from the Chawang beach road to the main island road. It has a large and well stocked bar, a fair sized dance floor with a good cross section of music and a stage with occasional live bands.

SEVEN

Naton

Anyone not flying to the island will find themselves at some point in Naton the capital, which is made up of three parallel streets. Although it's only a small town, the Samuians have managed to squeeze in three banks, two supermarkets, a dozen or so bars, restaurants and a fair-sized market place.

Amenities in Naton

As far as town life goes, Naton is pretty quiet after 6pm, when most of the tourist directed bars/restaurants close down. These days Naton does not lure people to the town as it once did, for the simple reason that, apart from the ferry (boats to Surat Thani and Koh Phangan), all the town's amenities can now be found on most parts of the island. However, there are a number of good reasons for visiting Samui's main town.

At the most southern point of Naton on First Street, near the Pha Ngan restaurant, is the **tourist police station**. Head north up First Street, passing the numerous travel offices, and half-way up is the **pier** where the ferries embark and disembark. Continue north to the **bus stand**, and finally the **main post office** is as far north up First Street as possible. This is a useful place to have mail sent, as they have an efficient poste-restante service which holds mail for up to two months. The address for this is: Post-Restante Naton, Koh Samui, Surat Thani. Overseas telephone calls can also be made from the main post office, the cost of a call being

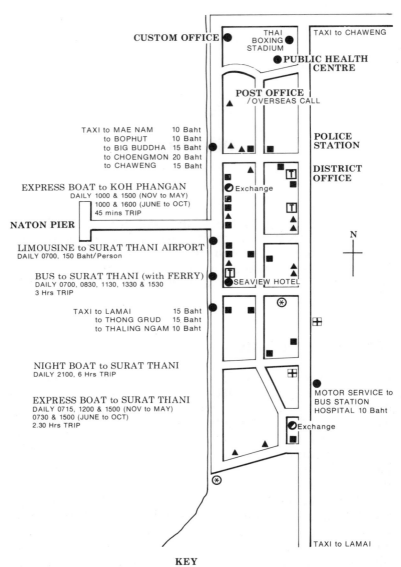

CUSTOM OFFICE

THAI BOXING STADIUM

TAXI to CHAWENG

PUBLIC HEALTH CENTRE

POST OFFICE /OVERSEAS CALL

TAXI to MAE NAM 10 Baht
to BOPHUT 10 Baht
to BIG BUDDHA 15 Baht
to CHOENGMON 20 Baht
to CHAWENG 15 Baht

POLICE STATION

DISTRICT OFFICE

EXPRESS BOAT to KOH PHANGAN
DAILY 1000 & 1500 (NOV to MAY)
1000 & 1600 (JUNE to OCT)
45 mins TRIP

NATON PIER

Exchange

N

LIMOUSINE to SURAT THANI AIRPORT
DAILY 0700, 150 Baht/Person

BUS to SURAT THANI (with FERRY)
DAILY 0700, 0830, 1130, 1330 & 1530
3 Hrs TRIP

SEAVIEW HOTEL

TAXI to LAMAI 15 Baht
to THONG GRUD 15 Baht
to THALING NGAM 10 Baht

NIGHT BOAT to SURAT THANI
DAILY 2100, 6 Hrs TRIP

MOTOR SERVICE to BUS STATION HOSPITAL 10 Baht

EXPRESS BOAT to SURAT THANI
DAILY 0715, 1200 & 1500 (NOV to MAY)
0730 & 1500 (JUNE to OCT)
2.30 Hrs TRIP

Exchange

TAXI to LAMAI

KEY

- ■ TRAVEL AGENT
- ⊞ CLINIC
- ◑ CURRENCY EXCHANGE SERVICE
- ⌶ LONG-DISTANCE TELEPHONE
- ⊛ JEEPS for RENT (500 Baht/24 Hrs)
- ▲ MOTORCYCLES for RENT (150-250 Baht/24 Hrs.)

NATON TOWN

cheaper than anywhere else on the island; but there can sometimes be a bit of a wait, as this service, although efficiently run, is much used by travellers. Opening times are 8.30am to noon and 1pm to 4.40pm. Behind the post office, on Middle Street, is the **immigration office.**

On Third Street, half-way up is a good **doctor's surgery.** Also on Third Street, at its southern end, is the **dentist.** Both doctor and dentist have a high standard of treatment. There is also a main **petrol station** in Third Street.

Shopping

Of course, one of the main attractions of any town are the shopping facilities, and Naton is no exception. Speaking in relative terms, shopping for clothes, artifacts and jewellery on the island is not too cheap, but by Western standards, goods can be purchased at a reasonable price.

Music tapes, for instance (fair quality pirates), can be bought for around 60 baht. The infamous Bangkok pirating business keeps Thailand up-to-date music-wise, and fairly recent titles can be found. There are a number of stalls and shops dotted around Naton selling these tapes, so finding them will not present any problem.

Between the Middle and Third streets, one can find numerous shops selling fashionable clothes at around half the Western prices. Traditional clothes and artifacts are to be found in abundance, but to any travellers who are heading to the north of Thailand (Chang Mai), the same items will be found at much cheaper prices. Please try your hand at bartering for goods; prices are flexible, especially when buying in quantity.

In Third Street, there are two large supermarkets, selling everything from safety pins to bottles of Scotch. Western food and beverages can be found here, and most goods are slightly cheaper than the shops on the rest of the island.

Also on Third Street is Samui's morning **market,** open Monday to Saturday until the early afternoon. Fruit, vegetables and fish are sold here. There is also a stall selling typically Thai food from 10 baht which is well worth sampling, but beware — it is hot!

Another good reason to visit Naton is to take advantage of the numerous **tailors and dressmakers** situated on Third Street. Garments can be made to measure at reasonable prices — allow up to a week for most items.

Towards evening, Naton becomes a town for the locals. The main activity is around the **port area**, where fishing vessels bring in their catch. For fresh seafood fanatics, this is the place to be. Everything from shrimp to shark can be purchased cheaply from the shore-loading fishermen on the front. The proprietor of your bungalow will cook your purchase for a small charge.

Eating out

Restaurants and eating houses are in abundance in Naton, but most close towards the evening. Should you find yourself in the town at this time, a nice spot for a meal and/or a drink is the **Pha Ngan** restaurant at the south end of First Street. Here, the menu is cheap, offering many and varied dishes, but the restaurant's main attraction is the fine sunset which can be easily viewed from here.

For those wishing to have an evening meal in Naton, there is **The Fountain**, a good Italian restaurant situated half-way up Middle Road, or the **El Pirata** at the north end of Middle Road, specialising in Spanish food. Beer and wine can be purchased at both places.

Close to the El Pirata is the **Golden Lion Pub**, which opens until midnight and just around the corner on Third Street is the fairly new **Eden Pub**, easily recognised by the front end of a car jutting out above the door. All beers and spirits can be found at both establishments.

After midnight, the **Pan On Café** at the south end of Middle Street is open until the early hours. This is, however, a rather expensive and flashy Thai night club.

Accommodation

For those wishing to stay overnight in Naton, there is the **Palace Hotel** in First Street, a little to the right of the pier, with rooms around 150-200 baht, and a restaurant down-stairs. Next door is Naton's cheapest hotel; it has no sign and rooms are from 45 baht (See also Accommodation Listings, Appendix 1). This place is also used as a brothel, so be warned.

EIGHT

Beaches and sea

Typically tropical beaches are in abundance on Samui. Most Samui beaches are covered with fine white sand and framed by a forest of coconut trees.

For those looking for night life, such as bars, restaurants and discos, Chaweng and Lamai might be the answer. For absolute rest, calm, peace and tranquillity, there are plenty of smaller, more secluded spots around the island.

Chaweng beach

This is the longest beach and, unfortunately, because of this fact, building there has intensified over the last couple of years. However, this does not mean that there is nowhere to find peace and quiet; on the contrary, towards the northern end of Chaweng, opposite the island of Matlang, little has changed and the mood is very tranquil. The very size of Chaweng makes it a good spot for those on a short vacation, simply because there is plenty of night life to be found south of Chaweng, but there is little entertainment at the north end of the beach.

The water is clear blue-green, and there are plenty of coral reefs for snorkelling enthusiasts and these are covered in depth in Chapter 10, Diving. Activities such as water skiing and wind surfing are also available.

Lamai beach

This is the second busiest beach. The actual area here is much smaller compared with Chaweng. The usual water sports and health activities can be found here, but its main "attraction" is its concentration of bars and restaurants around the beach, thus creating a blend of both day and night life.

Other beaches

For those seeking a quiet time, with few Western distractions, the beaches north, south and west of the island should be tried.

Mae Nam, north of Chaweng, has a very pretty strip of beach with the usual white sand, and palm trees added, with a touch of local colour supplied by the fishermen of the area.

Bo Phut and **Big Buddha** along the north end are slightly more secluded; the water here is not as clear as at Chaweng or Lamai, however.

Hat Thong Yang, on the west side of the island, is very tranquil, but the price here for seclusion is a less attractive beach.

Just north and south of Naton, the main town of Samui, are many tiny beaches with bungalows where the only real activities to be found are eating, swimming and sunbathing. Basically, any cove or inlet with the slightest hint of a beach has a bungalow or bungalows for rent nowadays. These are covered in greater depth in Appendix 1.

The sea

The ocean around Samui is generally pretty calm, but the tides can be very misleading on occasions, and there may be rather fierce undercurrents early and late in the year. As yet, the islanders have no system of warning flags or lifeguards on the beaches, so there are tragic accidents now and then involving unaware visitors. However, ninety-five percent of the time, the sea is almost too passive.

Water scooters, wind surfers, catamarans and other such ocean vehicles can be hired on the two main beaches of Chaweng and Lamai, with the former also offering water skis for hire from Louis' Bakery, next to the OP Bungalows. Windsurfing facilities can also be found at Bo-Phut and Mae Nam. The water between the Malibu (which hires out surfers and catamarans) and Louis' (Chaweng) is normally extremely calm, being bordered by a natural reef, and it is thus a good location for beginners.

NINE

Sightseeing

Waterfalls

There are two waterfalls on the island: Hin Lad and Na Muang, both being well worth a visit.

To reach **Hin Lad Waterfall**, one must take the 4169 route out of Naton towards Lamai. Within a couple of kilometres the 4172 road will appear, crossing the main road; turn left down it to bring you to the base of the fall.

Here it is a good idea to take refreshments and have a quick dip in the pool, before ascending the jungle climb, a walk of about half an hour, give or take ten minutes. A small stopping-off platform has recently been erected a few hundred metres up; it is well worth resting here a few minutes to take in not only the cold drinks which are sold but also the very pretty scenery.

Continuing upward along a narrow path will take you through tropical jungle foliage and past many trees of great age and splendour. The path can be a little tricky in places, but is not too difficult for the average person. Once you reach the top, the magnificent waterfall, which can be a few hundred feet across in certain seasons, will come into view. When taken with its surroundings, it makes a truly spectacular scene.

After the long climb, bathing here is most refreshing, and occasionally there is a man selling cold drinks. But do not rely upon his appearing, as he only does so when the mood takes him.

Na-Muang Waterfall is further on down the 4169 road to where, about ten kilometres from Naton, the attractive

Phallung Restaurant stands on the left. Follow the left turn along its pleasant, windy way for a few hundred metres, and the waterfall will come into view. Although it is very small compared to Hin Lad, it is still very pretty and provides an excellent place for a picnic, being a good bathing spot where cool refreshments and souvenirs can be bought.

Samui Highland Park

Back on the 4169 road, just past the Hin Lad turn-off, is the trail for Samui Highland Park. The climb to the highest point one can reach is about two hours through a rubber plantation with expanses of vegetation and wild flowers along the way.

The park was built by a man called Khun Kosol, probably now in his sixties, who takes his mule to the top each morning to say hello to visitors, offer them some refreshment and to look after his property.

He built his retreat apparently to resemble the Genting Highlands in Malaysia and it was opened to the public in honour of H.M. the King on his sixtieth birthday in 1987.

The panoramic view from the park makes the climb well worth it for enthusiasts, but we strongly recommend making an early morning start as climbing in the Samui heat is somewhat uncomfortable to say the least. Leave the park a couple of hours before sunset, as a descent at night is perilous with a good flashlight, and impossible without one.

The Marine National Park

At the turn-off for Tong Yang harbour, where the Don Sak car ferry is situated, on the Naton-Lamai route on the 4169, is Tong Yang Bay.

Whilst the beaches here are not the best, the sunsets over the dragon-spined Ang Thong Marine National Park must be among the most beautiful anywhere.

The Park can be visited by glass-bottomed boat from

Naton Pier — times vary — or see Chaweng Gardens, Chaweng, for details.

Wats

Thailand is indeed a land of many monasteries or Wats, as they are known there (see also Chapter 3, Religion), and they vary greatly in splendour, size and interest. However we have to say that we did not find these religious buildings on the island to hold much attraction when compared to the ones we saw in Bangkok, which are teeming with life, monks, ceremonies, numerous offering altars and which house schools of learning, dance, massage and music. Most of the Wats on Koh Samui are devoid of the usual opulent Buddhist artifacts and relics such as statues and wall paintings and are no more than extremely simple shell-like buildings with little or no decor to catch the eye. Some are just large platforms on stilts with roofs.

The only Wat of any interest is the one at Big Buddha beach. This huge modern image of Buddha is visible from quite a distance, being about 12 metres high, and is a beautiful sight as is sits overlooking the sea, particularly at sunset. To get to **Big Buddha** (as it is known simply on the island) take the 4169 towards Bo Phut beach and turn right going down the airport road before entering the town and you will see it looming up long before you reach the place.

It is surrounded by lush greenery and the huge Buddha presides at the top of some steep steps that are guarded at the bottom by two huge colourful and angry looking warrior statues. The entrance to the Wat is actually at the base of the Buddha's feet; inside is fairly spartan and not particularly thrilling, but the monks here do welcome visitors. There are a few handicraft stalls and food and drink cafés as you walk up to the enclosure and if you ask around you will even discover a fortune teller, if that is what takes your fancy.

The only other fairly interesting temple is **Wat Laem Saw**, which is at the southern tip of the island near the village of Bang Kao and has an interesting pagoda.

Other places to visit

Ban Taling Ngam, with its nearby beach and good view of the mainland, has lots of granite rocks dotting its coast. The best known formation in the area is the rocky Ko Si Ko Ha Islets, which literally means "Four of Five Islands".

Further south on Highway 4170, an off-the-beaten-track path, is **Ban Tong Tanot**, a rocky point with caves nearby and boat access to the castaway islands called Koh Tan, Koh Mudson and Koh Katen.

Travelling on another ten kilometres from here, Highway 4170 passes through **Ban Thale** village, past an old Chinese house and a revered Buddha footprint.

Back on the 4169 Lamai main road, the village of **Ban Sa Ket** is reached. Here, traditional fishing life, Thai style, goes on the same as it has for centuries, authentic and unaltered.

A few kilometres further, passing through paddy fields along the way, brings you to the village of **Hua Thanon**, a small, bustling Chinese community. This is quite an interesting little place also housing a group of Muslim fishermen, situated in Koh Samui's one and only ghetto-type area. Here, too, can be found the Natta guest house, which offers dormitory rooms for thirty baht per person. Coral blocks carved in Buddha's image can be found in this area, only two hundred metres from the main road in tall grass on the left-hand side.

One curiosity just south of Lamai Vane at **Hin Yai** are the strange rock formations known as the Grandmother and Grandfather rocks, because of their uncanny resemblance to the female and male genitals.

Overlap Stone is just off the 4169 on the road to Lamai, and from this viewpoint can be seen yet another panoramic scene. Absolute enthusiasts can even trek through fairly heavy-going jungle all the way to the **Samui Highlands** from here; allow half a day and avoid setting off in the daytime heat.

For the less adventurous, there is a small restaurant a few thousand metres up a rocky path, where also can be found bungalows for day-rent. A very basic one costs about sixty baht, but better ones are available. The view from this point is great, overlooking as it does a fantastic bay. If you want to get away from the beach for a while, there is no better place than here; descending after sunset is pretty precarious, so why not enjoy a good meal and a couple of beers, sample a glass of Mekong, and relax. Many people spend the night here, and set off early the next day towards the highlands.

TEN

Things to do

Meditation

Courses are offered at the **Garden Home Herbal Health Centre** two kilometres north of Naton, specialising in the wellbeing of body and mind and offering a number of options designed to suit the participant, ranging from soothing, herbal massage to deep concentration of the mind.

There is also a monastery at **Wat Pangbua**, in the northern part of Chaweng, which runs ten-day courses. Take the Chaweng beach road to the OP Bungalows, turn left down the new road and, a few hundred yards along on the right, you will see the Wat sign-posted. Here the monks may or may not make charges, depending upon their financial position at the time. However, when charges are made they are minimal and include the cost of food. Total silence must be observed, and the participant is not allowed to leave the beautiful monastic gardens. Meditation techniques are taught. Early rising and restricted eating are the rules, and many people leave long before the ten days are completed. These courses normally start at the beginning of each calendar month and are open to both men and women.

(Opposite, top) *It is a long climb to Hin Lad Waterfall and you can reward yourself with a refreshing bathe.*

(Opposite, bottom) *Naton, the capital, is quite small but you'll find banks, supermarkets, bars, restaurants and market-place there, as well as the ferry pier.*

(Opposite, top and bottom) *Most Samui beaches have fine white sand and are fringed by palm tress.*

(Above) *Fresh fruit, as in this wonderful display, as well as vegetables and fish are sold in the market and typically Thai food (very hot!) is also on sale.*

Silangu, a naturally tranquil place giving substance to the Buddhist doctrine of peace and non-violence, lies between Hua Thanon and Lamai. It has a venerated Pagoda, reputed to enshrine a bone fragment of the Buddha; traditional Vispassana meditation courses are held here several times a year, and foreigners are invited to attend.

Museums

There are two "museums" in Koh Samui so far; we do not think either of them are worth a special visit to see, but if you are in the locality, pop in. At the Wat in Lamai is the small **Memorabilia Museum**, next to the Lamai Cultural Hall. Of interest here is a 480-year old ceramic jar, salvaged from a sunken wreck off Koh Samui.

The second museum is situated in the south-west corner of Samui, off the 4170 road heading towards Ban Thong Tanot, in one of the local schools, where a small contribution may be made (totally voluntary). Known as a **Marine Museum**, there is no room to swing a cat here, but we think it is the more interesting of the two, with its exhibits of various sea creatures, all to be found living in the Gulf of Thailand, preserved in sealed jars of alcohol. All but the Aussies might have second thoughts about swimming too far out after seeing some of these monsters, creatures like stone fish and other ugly and dangerous underwater dwellers!

(Opposite, top) *In Thai boxing, the boxers may use fists for punching, feet and knees for kicking and pushing, and elbows for jabbing. They may strike any part of their opponent's body.*

(Opposite, bottom) *These children were delighted to pose for our photo. The Thais love children and visitors taking their own children will find that life is made as easy as possible for them.*

Cycling

This opens up a host of possibilities, and there are a number of places around the island hiring out pushbikes (no tandems as of yet) from 60-100 baht per day. The following bike tour will take anything from between half a day to one day depending on your chosen pace, we would say take a whole day to enjoy it.

If you start your tour in the main town of Naton and head in a southerly direction for about three kilometres the first stop is the **Hin Lad Waterfall** which is the first turning on the left by the hospital and is signposted. At the end of the forest lined road there is a small lake, where sometimes you will be lucky enough to see one of the monkeys trained to climb coconut trees and pick the fruit taking a bath there. To the right of the lake there is the signposted route to the waterfall, it's about a 30 minute walk but well worth the effort to get to the cool shady fall where the first thing you will do will probably be to plunge your feet into the refreshing clear water. All along the route is thick tropical vegetation. There is also a small Buddhist **temple** to the left of the lake at the entrance, which is surrounded by lush gardens and is worth a 10 minute stop.

Back onto the main road going south for about seven kilometres you will come to (on the left) **Na-Muang Waterfall**. You can cycle all the way up to this fall and there are usually a couple of makeshift drinks and fresh fruit stalls at the entrance. This waterfall is the prettier of the two and one can have a swim and stand behind the fall — very refreshing.

Onto route 4170 and if you veer off to the right between the two waterfalls this road will take you down to the southernmost point of the island where there is a **pagoda** sitting at the edge of the water; this is a tranquil stop before going on to Lamai beach.

Lamai beach is one of the favourites on the island, and has quite a lively village too (though it is full of Western bars and restaurants — not very Thai). There's a cultural hall which was established by the monks and has lots of information about the islanders and their culture. There are also two very realistic and virile looking rock formations named Grandma and Grandpa stone. You will see why when you take a look and they are not likenesses of an elderly couple!

Continue along the coast and you will come to **Coral Cove**, with wonderful panoramic views of Chaweng beach and Coral Bay. Then along to **Big Buddha beach** and the **Big Buddha** statue, which dominates the skyline on Koh Fau, a tiny island with a meditation centre and linked by a causeway. The road then continues along the coast going through **Bophut**, which has an interesting village, to Maenam beach and around and back to Naton once more.

All along the way there are numerous dirt tracks and paths made by the islanders and one can spend many hours meandering through the coconut groves.

Diving

Diving courses and snorkelling are comparatively cheap in Koh Samui, and two courses are available to obtain either a NAVI (National Association Underwater Instructors) or a PADI (Professional Association Diving Instructors). Addresses for these are:

Koh Samui Divers Head Office, Angthong Road (Middle Road), Naton, Tel: 421465

Malibu Beach Club Chaweng, Postal address: PO Box 1, Koh Samui, Thailand.

The costs of the basic NAVI and PADI courses, including five main dives in main water, are around 6500 baht, plus 500 baht for a day trip to the National Marine Park. A two-day trip to Koh Tao is an extra 1000 baht, whilst a three day trip will cost about 1500 baht. Food and accommodation are included in the trip prices.

Koh Tao (Turtle Island) is a beautiful island, surrounded by coral reefs, with an amazing variety of underwater plant and animal life. This is a really good way to learn to dive in picturesque surroundings. Snorkelling trips to Koh Tao are run simultaneously, and are also inclusive of food and accommodation.

Other diving trips to the island, which include equipment hire, boat, food, accommodation and at least two dives a day, cost 3200 baht for two days and one night, and 4300 baht for three days and two nights.

Day trips to the National Marine Park, including equipment, boat, two dives and lunch cost 1900 baht, and the same deal around Koh Samui costs 1500 baht. One beach dive is 450 baht, and a night dive 750 baht.

Other dive courses are available at the following prices:

	Advanced	Rescue	Divemaster
NAVI	7000 baht	5500 baht	12000 baht
PADI	6000 baht	5500 baht	12000 baht

If you are really into diving or snorkelling, then **Fantasea Diving and Yachting** (Swiss Country Club Travel, 41 Na-Amphur Road, Tel: 077 421538) has got to be the place for you, with its calm waters, beautiful setting and cheap prices. PADI certificates can be obtained here, and these people organise trips of all sorts, costing 2000 baht for one day's diving, 3800 baht for two days, 5000 baht for three days. Beach diving will cost you 1300 baht. Food and transport are included in the prices.

Fishing trips are organised including deep sea fishing for 1500 baht, bottom and net fishing for 1000 baht and shark fishing (two days) for 4000 baht. Snorkelling off boat costs 600 baht, whilst sailing and snorkelling on a junk costs 800 baht.

The same company also arranges visits to see monkeys working on the coconut trees, knocking down the ripened fruits — probably of more interest to children than adults. Air conditioned mini-buses depart from the Fantasea office at 1pm approximately and cost 150 baht per person.

Prices quoted may vary slightly, but will serve as a good guideline.

Thai boxing

There are a few places on the island to see Thai boxing *(muay Thai)* just outside Naton, in Lamai and on Chaweng. Sometimes boxing rings are set up in clearings, so keep an eye out for the numerous posters which spring up. Small vans with loud speakers go around announcing forthcoming fights, but normally in the Thai language, although you will know what they are about from the pictures or cardboard cutouts of boxers fixed to their sides.

Places like the **Flamingo** in Lamai and some of the bigger resorts around the island hold tournaments, but these "fights" are more for show than actual contest, although tournaments with mainland challengers are usually real.

To the foreigner, the strange rules, or apparent lack of rules, may seem quite amazing. Like their Western counterparts, two fighters wearing robes, baggy versions of boxing shorts, and twelve or sixteen ounce gloves enter the ring followed by their trainers. There the similarities end; the boxers are barefoot and wear an armband around their biceps, with an amulet sewn in.

An interesting ritual precedes each bout; wailing music issues forth, usually from a small orchestra but sometimes pre-recorded, the instruments being a Java pipe (similar in sound to a discordant bagpipe), two drums and a pair of cymbals. To the accompaniment of this eerie sound, the two contestants kneel with hands together, raise their heads and bow three times to the floor, thus paying homage to their teachers and praying to the spirits for protection and victory. They then perform a strange dance of perfect timing and balance in time to the slow tempo of the music. This form of "limbering up" is also meant to be intimidating to the opponent. Each boxer wears a *mongkon* in a loop on his head; this is a sacred cord which has been consecrated by his own teacher, and it is removed at the end of the ritual dance.

The boxers shake hands, and the fight begins; the music speeds up as the tension rises; throughout the bout, the drums beat faster and the pipes wail with increasing gusto, as the boxers respond by pounding and kicking each other with rising frenzy. They are allowed to use their fists for punching, their feet and knees for kicking and pushing, and their elbows for jabbing. They may strike any part of the body. Contests are over five three-minute rounds, with two-minute rests between each.

In some parts of Thailand — Bangkok, Pattaya and Phuket for example — visitors are invited to try their luck in the ring. All we can say is, do not underestimate these boxers; they are fit, fast and extremely tough. They may occasionally be shamming with each other in the ring, but they will not be doing so with you!

Thai boxing developed years ago from combat training; media publicity brought the once secret martial art to the forefront. In its early day, this hard and fast method of combat was extremely dangerous, even when the ancient art of war had developed into a highly exciting spectator sport. Up to one in three fights ended in the death of one of the contestants, and the most lethal blow, the elbow strike to the temple, is now banned.

Prior to the 1930s, when rules and regulations were introduced, contestants would get into a ring wearing crude boxing gloves made of hemp, which had often been dipped into a mixture of glue and ground glass, producing horrific results.

Buffalo fighting

A new buffalo "stadium" has been erected between Naton and Ban Thurian, although the word "stadium" is used in a very loose context, as it actually comprises a wide square field, surrounded by crude fencing. There are some seating arrangements, although most people stand round the field. There is another such place at Chaweng just off the 4169 road.

Buffalo fighting is a seasonal affair. Basically, two male water buffalo are tied to stakes in a field. The area around them becomes, after a time, their territory, where they urinate and excrete. The "twist" is that the Thais erect a makeshift curtain between the two animals, who remain oblivious to each other's presence. An hour or so before the fight is due to begin, the owners or "trainers" of the beasts spray them with more of their own urine, thus emphasising territory, and certain stimulating fluids are then forced down the animals' throats. If you arrive early enough, you will notice that the buffalo are fairly docile, normally just lying around with complete lack of interest in their surroundings. However, after the masters have finished their preparations, the animals are in a much agitated state. When, on the sound of a bell, the dividing curtain is raised and each buffalo is released, the sight of another male in his territory infuriates each bull, and they attack each other until one of them flees through a specially erected exit. The whole "sport" centres mainly around the proceeds of the widespread gambling which takes place on each fight.

We visited one such event in Chaweng, where the handlers of one of the bulls grabbed a horn each and forced the animal to charge forward just as the dividing curtain was being raised. The opposing bull was so surprised and bewildered by the unexpected charge that he simply high-tailed and ran for the exit. But our experience was only one fight; there are many ghastly stories of gouged-out eyes and other severe, gory injuries, even tales of bulls charging into the spectators. So, all in all, animal lovers and the squeamish (such as us) are advised to stay well away.

Cockfighting

This is another gruesome sport organised around gambling for the local men, who normally hold fights every Saturday. Razor-sharp blades are attached to the cocks' feet, and two of them are thrown into a ring. Fighting is bloody, and the first bird to leave the space designated as the arena (if still alive) is the loser. Very few *farangs* are invited to these affairs but, if you are so inclined, you can probably get a local to take you along. Many local men find this barbaric practice most exhilarating — we think it best that they keep it among themselves.

Fishing

Fishing trips are advertised in a lot of the many larger resorts, mostly through **Swiss Country Club Travel** (41 Na-Amphur Road, Tel: 077 421538). However, many locals around the island also organise morning, afternoon or day trips, usually for around 200 baht. These are great fun; equipment and bait are supplied, and it is advisable to take along cold beers or drinks in a cold storage box.

A narrow boat of about ten metres in length with a simple but effective motor is the vessel which carries the would-be fisher out to sea. The locals know the best spots, and even complete novices will usually catch a fish or two. In the evening, upon request and for a small extra payment, the day's catch can be cooked with various spices by the fisherman's family.

It is a fantastic way to spend the day, and one of the nicest trips we experienced was from Louis' Bakery on Chaweng beach, opposite Koh Matlang, a very small island at the north end of Chaweng. The trip took us around the far side of Matlang Island, where fish seem to abound in the tranquil setting.

Snooker

There are a few snooker tables on the island. On the 4169 between Chaweng and Naton, look out for the **Dove** snooker halls; there are two, one on the right of the road just outside Chaweng, heading towards Naton, the other just off the 4169 on the left in Mae Nam, heading towards Naton. There is only one table in each, neither in particularly good condition, but playable. Games cost just 10 baht. The halls are open twenty-four hours, and beer, drinks and food are available until the early evening, and sometimes all night.

The **Flamingo** and **Chicago** discos have snooker tables which leave a lot to be desired, but those players not too fussy about the condition of the table will be able to get a game there.

Massage

There are so-called masseuses and occasionally a masseur who roam the main beaches, offering massage at 100 baht per hour; we are somewhat dubious about their qualifications. Should you decide to use one of these people, we recommend that you ask for a gentle massage, as they can be very vigorous indeed, and anyone with sprains, pulled muscles or worse would be well advised to avoid them altogether.

A good traditional Thai massage can be obtained at the **Garden Home Herbal Health Centre**, which is just two kilometres north of Naton, and is quite well sign-posted. Their advertisement reads "Good health and vitality is your most precious asset. At our herbal centre, we provide true healing in natural, peaceful surroundings. For your general well-being or for specific health problems, we have a health programme using healing herbs, special herbal teas, herbal steam therapy and professional Thai massage." The centre is open every day of the week between 9am and 5pm, and prices start from about 200 baht.

Another reputable masseuse specialising in ancient Thai massage is on **Chaweng Noi** beach, near the Imperial Samui Hotel. Here again, charges are from about 200 baht.

ELEVEN

Island hopping excursions

There are two islands in the area well worth a visit: Koh
Phangan and Koh Tao.

Koh Phangan

Koh Phangan is 14 kilometres from Samui, and is reached
by boat either from Naton Pier at 10am and 3pm, or Bo
Phut at 9.30am and 3pm. The island is (or at least, was)
much more primitive that Samui, with no roads; just dirt
tracks run the circumference of the place. It remains
typically tropical and very peaceful and tranquil in the
main.

The sunsets on "Sunset" side of Phangan are the best we
have seen anywhere in the world (even better than Bali).
The entire spectrum of colours accompany the event,
making it a truly breathtaking experience; a sight not to be
missed!

A further boat trip takes you to the northern part of the
island, which is of a completely different appearance, surrounded as it is by pine trees, of all things. It is a nice little
retreat.

The main town, **Thong Sala**, houses a bank and post
office. Motor bikes run as taxis, the riders being amazingly
skilled handling their machines; two of us and our luggage
were carried with the greatest of ease.

The best south to north road is from Thong Sala to
Chalok Lum, a fishing village on the north coast. It passes
through the centre of the island, and offers grand vistas of

the mountainous interior. From Chalok Lum to Bottle Beach, a favourite hideaway beach with bungalows, you must take a boat or walk overland on the beach path.

Another road from Thong Sala heads southeast along the shore, and ends at **Baan Khaay**, where boats depart for **Haadrin Beach**. The boat trip from Baan Khaay takes about thirty minutes, and costs 50 baht. Haadrin can also be reached from Bo Phut on Koh Samui, with boats leaving 9.30am and 3pm (check times, as they frequently change). All boat trips on the island are subject to weather conditions.

Shortly before Baan Khaay, near the village of Baan Tai, is an unimproved road, which heads north through the centre of the island to **Thong Thaa Paan Beach**, which was once the favourite of King Rama V. From this royal holiday resort, boats make the trip north to Bottle Beach or south to Haadrin.

Haadrin is the one exception to the tranquil atmosphere of the remainder of the island; it is the new Goa beach, with wild parties being thrown every full moon, that go on till daybreak and are attended mainly by the new "designer hippy" types. "Conversation" revolves quite frequently around drugs and the best places to find them, which we found to be an extremely boring topic and very old hat. Just at this time, unfortunately, Haadrin is inhabited almost permanently by the drug escapists, which is a great shame because the locale really is a beauty-spot, now being ruined by manic building and steep prices. There is a good outdoor disco, the Casablanca, catering for a wide selection of music tastes, open until very late.

Koh Tao

Koh Tao is the original remote tropical island. Every Monday, Wednesday and Friday, a boat leaves from Bo Phut Bay on Samui at 9.30, reaching Ko Phangan at Chalok Lum Bay at 11am, and sailing on to Koh Tao, arriving at **Mae Haad** at 1.30. For tickets, contact Koh Tao Travel at 25/1 Bo Phut, Koh Samui.

There is not much to do as far as entertainment goes but it is a great retreat, with beautiful coral and clear waters, perfect for scuba diving, snorkelling or just swimming. Here, you can truly relax.

Be careful, however, in the wetter seasons, as ferry crossings can be positively dangerous and people have drowned. A friend of ours spent forty minutes clinging to the side of a capsized ferry, convinced he was about to meet his maker; thankfully, rescue came, and he, along with about twenty others, was taken back to Tao until the storms subsided a few days later.

TWELVE

General information

Drugs

Many people head for Asia specifically for drug-related reasons. We would warn them very strongly of the risks they are taking. Dealers can be particularly unscrupulous, figuring that most of their customers are transient and plentiful. All sorts of noxious substances are liberally mixed, and can be extremely dangerous, with drug-related deaths being more than common in this part of the world. In addition, drug users risk getting into trouble with the law. The one-time relaxed attitude to drug-taking is now very much a thing of the past, and police are under orders to stamp out even the smoking of marijuana.

Health

There are no statutory requirements for Samui, which is a pretty "safe" place to travel in healthwise, although the neighbouring island of Phangan has been known to have occasional (albeit rare) outbreaks of malaria. Health vaccinations are at the individual's discretion but, bearing in mind that this is South-east Asia, it would be prudent to check with your doctor or 'phone your Thai embassy before travelling, while taking out travel sickness insurance is always a good idea. In addition, there are a small number of precautions and safeguards which the wise visitor to Samui will take.

- As in all Asian countries, avoid drinking tap water. Use only bottled waters, and ice bought from factories where it is made up of purified water.
- Cuts should be treated immediately, as they can often rapidly develop into tropical ulcers. It is wise to pack a small bottle of disinfectant or some antiseptic cream when going to Samui, as the powders and creams on sale locally are often useless.
- Avoid sea-bathing with any open cuts or grazes; plenty of germs can hang around the waters of the tropics just waiting to pounce into an unsuspecting wound, and the old theory of salt water being a great antiseptic healer certainly does not apply in Samui.

There are pharmacies and clinics dotted around the island, specifically equipped to deal with tropical ulcers; however, because these places make money from whatever pills and so-called antibiotics they can sell, they will "prescribe" as many products as possible, and these may be so weak as to be ineffectual, or so potent as to cause dire side-effects. It is often much wiser to take the time to visit a hospital instead. The **Catholic clinic** on the Chaweng-Naton Road in Chaweng has a very good reputation for treating cuts, grazes and ulcers, as does the **clinic in Naton**, opposite the market on the main road. Here, a consultation will cost two hundred baht, plus the cost of medicines. There is also a small **hospital** two kilometres from Naton, going towards Lamai (telephone number: Surat Thani 272331).

Now and then, the occasional bug will sweep through Samui, causing either an influenza-type of aching in the bones, or a brief spell of diarrhoea, and normally lasting only a day or so. The usual treatment is to avoid food and have a day of fluid intake only. If hunger pains become overwhelming, a temporary diet of salted white rice and black tea can help. Medical aid should be sought if any symptoms persist as constant diarrhoea may be a sign of dysentery, which will require treatment with the correct antibiotics.

Sunburn

Please take adequate precautions to prevent sunburn and heatstroke; the sun is extremely hot after 11am until as late as 4pm. About twenty to thirty minutes is the longest one should stay out in the direct sun for the first few days without a high factor sun protection cream. A hat is also a good idea and is essential for children.

Taking the children

Thailand is one country in which travelling with children can actually be a great asset. The Thais love children and will often go out of their way to make young ones feel at home, showering them with sweets and goodies. The Thais will make life as easy as possible for parents with children, and in many cases the under-tens will not be charged for accommodation.

The main things to be aware of are sunburn and occasionally rough sea waters. Otherwise, the idyllic beach life of Samui is perfect for mums and dads who just want to let the kids get on with it with minimum fuss.

There are no real facilities geared towards children as such, but the natural surroundings should provide plenty of entertainment. Shallow pools of sea water hold tiny marine life, where colourful rocks, plants and even small fish can be observed or collected. A trip to watch the monkeys picking coconuts is always fascinating for children.

Cheating

A word of warning: like anywhere else, South East Asia being no exception, cheating is an unfortunate occurrence. Please exercise caution, especially with the taxi drivers.

Time difference

Thailand is seven hours ahead of GMT Summertime and eight hours ahead of Wintertime.

Renewing visas

If you obtained a non-immigrant tourist visa (see Chapter 1, Documentation section) which is due to expire and you wish to stay longer you can apply for a renewal at the visa office which is situated behind the post office in Naton town. This is very easy to find, just ask. It is open from 9am to 5pm weekdays only with lunch closure being at any time between 12pm and 2pm. The office is closed weekends and bank holidays.

You may initially apply for a further 30 days. The fee is 500 baht and you need two photographs which can also be obtained at the same office. You can then go back and obtain a further 15 day visa costing 500 baht and 2 more photographs but be warned, the staff at the visa office do not like extensive paperwork involved with an already expired visa, and an extension will probably be refused if renewal is not made in good time.

Anyone wishing to extend a tourist visa beyond the periods stated or apply for a non-immigrant tourist visa after their 15 day transit visa has expired must make the day long trip to Penang in Malaysia (the easiest destination) where a new visa can be purchased with the minimum of fuss. We could never find out why one has to actually leave the country to obtain a new visa. We can only assume this is an economically profitable arrangement between the two countries.

The most popular method of getting to Penang from Koh Samui is to take the night ferry for about 60 baht to Surat Thani, leaving Naton at 9pm and arriving on the mainland at about 3am. Passengers are allowed to remain asleep on the ferry until 5.30am, at which time the buses or coaches leave for the 4-6 hours journey to Hat Yai, from where mini-buses and taxis can be taken to Penang, about 5-7 hours away. As the Malaysian border closes at 5pm, travellers are advised to leave Hat Yai no later than 2.30pm. Including the night ferry fare, the whole journey costs about 450-500 baht, one way.

Once in Penang, most travellers make their way to Chulia Street, if their bus or taxi has not already dropped them off there, as it is full of a great variety of guest houses and hotels costing from as little as nine Malaysian dollars (90 baht) upwards.

The following morning, a number 7 bus takes the traveller directly to the Thai Embassy; it is wise to plan your arrival there for as near 9am as possible. Passports must be left there together with three photographs which can be obtained at several shops in Chulia Street, and the fee of about thirty Malaysian dollars (300 baht), and may be collected that same afternoon. The Embassy closes for lunch from noon to 2pm, and is then open until 4pm.

Some hotels will take your passport to the embassy for you, obtain your visa and collect it again the same day. They charge a small fee for this service which you may find worth paying as it leaves you the day free to explore Penang. You can also hire a rickshaw which is a pleasant, relaxing way to travel or take a taxi.

Buses direct to Thailand leave from 4am onwards every morning, and can be booked in a multitude of places around Chulia Street.

The main reasons for the popularity of this itinerary are that the night ferry offers mattresses, enabling a good night's sleep, without the added expense of an extra night's accommodation, and also the fact that one can be back in Koh Samui within three days.

Tax

Anyone staying in Thailand more than 90 days in one calendar year has to obtain a tax clearance certificate from the tax office, and may still be liable to pay a minimum tax. This, together with the time and effort involved, can vary from town to town.

For instance, at Surat Thani a form has to be collected at one office, taken across town for payment of the fee or an official stamp, and then be returned to the original office, all of which can prove time consuming and frustrating. At Songkhla, however, the whole procedure can be completed within an hour.

Accommodation listings

A comprehensive list of accommodation, working around the island in a clockwise direction from the main town, follows. Note that all bungalows have a restaurant or café facility. These vary somewhat in the quality and range of food offered and the standard of service provided, so it is very much up to the visitor to hunt around and experiment.

Naton

Most people do not make a point of staying in Naton and for this reason accommodation in the main town is limited.
Palace Hotel Situated on the Naton front, close to the pier. Fairly basic accommodation. For an overnight stay, large rooms with fan and bathroom cost 200 baht. Large rooms with fan, bathroom and double bed cost 250 baht.
Sunset Bungalow Medsai: about ten minutes ride from Naton. Fair-sized bungalows with Western style toilets, for 200 baht a night. As implied by the name, a good place for a sunset.

Mae Nam Beach

Home Bay Resort A nice sheltered spot with raised wooden bungalows. Cheapies at 40 baht a night. 80 baht can get one with a basic shower, 150 baht gets their best bungalows.

Coco Palms Village Brick bungalows raised with a balcony, new and clean, all with private bathrooms. Single and double beds; overlooking a nice beach. 400 baht a night.
Shangrila Quiet setting on a pleasant beach. Raised wooden bungalows with own shower. 200 and 250 baht.
Mae Nam Resort Large wooden bungalows, with French windows leading onto a balcony overlooking the beach. Good value at 200 baht. Also has a pool table for anyone interested.
Lolitta Bungalows Wooden bungalows with a good selection, starting from 100 baht for shower, 200 baht double bed and shower, and 500 baht for very large with two rooms. Nice quiet beach setting.

Mae Nam Village

This is further along the 4169, a small, quaint place with a few cafés and bakeries. Overseas telephone calls can be made here. There is also a Buddhist temple (not worth getting too excited about). Three sets of bungalows in this area are worth noting.
Mae Nam Beach Bungalows Just right of the town, near the Homemade Bakery. 120 baht a night, with shower. Windsurfing here for 100 baht an hour.
Maen Hut A dozen or so bungalows of the wooden type. Good value for long stayers at 150 baht a night.
Seashore Bungalows A clean and compact site, close to the road. The bungalows are small with shower and fan for 100 baht a night. Electricity is on between 6pm and 6am.

Bo Phut

Bo Phut Guest House Small brick-type accommodation, with largish verandah and corrugated, just before the village of Bo Phut. Some bungalows are built on a swamp-like lake, so watch out for mosquitoes. Quite nice, however, all with shower, toilet and fans, costing 100, 150 and 200 baht.

World Bungalow (Tel: 077 421 355/6) Large new spacious bungalows made of brick and wood. Prices start at 200 baht, with shower, toilet and fan. 300 baht is the next price level, while 500 baht gets a very large room. Jeeps and motorbikes for hire. Overseas telephone service, money exchange and travel bookings. Geared for the holiday-maker.

Samui Palm Beach (Tel/Fax: 077 421 358) Twenty large brick bungalows with air conditioning. Nicely furnished and very comfortable, for 1500 baht, plus an extra 200 baht for a sea view, and another 300 baht for an extra bed.

Palm Garden Bungalow Brick and wooden type, with shower, toilet and fan. 150 baht. Boat trips organised to the coral islands.

Siam Sea Lodge (Tel: 077 421 360) Located off the beach, off the Bo Phut village road. A two-storey building set around a square, similar to a Spanish villa in appearance. Some bungalows are available, starting from 100 baht. New clean rooms with fan from 350 baht. Some rooms available with air conditioning, refrigerator and water heater — price determined on request.

Ziggy Stardust Next to Siam Sea Lodge. Average bungalows with shower, toilet and fan, 300 and 400 baht.

Smile House Comfortable bungalows of three different sizes; the larger the bungalow, the larger the price: 300,400 and 600 baht. Surrounds a swimming pool.

Boon Bungalow Very basic huts, situated on the road. Just a bed for 60 baht. Some are available with fan, shower and toilet for 150 baht.

Comos Also very basic huts, 50 to 60 baht. Unsheltered area.

Net Guest House Situated on the connecting road between the 4169 and Bo Phut village. Rooms are of the motel type, with fan and shower. Nice and clean, and relatively new. 150 baht per night.

Big Buddha

Take the 4171 road from Bo Phut to find the majority of bungalows in this area.

Champ Villa Has an Italian pizza restaurant and the Gi-Gi Bar. Fairly average bungalows for 350 baht a night.

L A Resort Wood and brick type buildings with shower, toilet and fan. 150 and 250 baht.

Big Buddha Bungalows Large, clean rooms, with tiled floor and a wardrobe to boot. Good value for accommodation and food. Rooms on the beach 150 and 200 baht. Close to airport so can be noisy at times but nothing too severe.

Nara Lodge (Tel: 077 421 364) Motel style accommodation, set right on the beach, overlooking the statue of Big Buddha. Clean and modern, good value. Air conditioned rooms with hot water, 950 baht. Air conditioned rooms 750 baht. Rooms with fans, 500 baht. Deep sea fishing. Windsurfing and island hopping tours. Thai, Chinese and European cuisine. Geared for the holiday-maker.

Farn Bay Resort Motel style rooms, with air conditioning. New, clean rooms at 1050 baht per night.

Thong Son Bay

Continuing along the 4171, just past the Big Buddha statue is the beginning of Thong Son Bay, where the beaches are mostly quiet and secluded. Many places are accessible only by jeep, motorbike or on foot. The advantage, of course, is that seclusion-seekers are virtually guaranteed peace and quiet.

Golden Pine Resort Set on a high level, overlooking the small Thong Son Bay. Medium sized wooden bungalows, five in all, with shower and toilet, 150 baht a night.

Thong Sai Bay Cottage Another secluded spot off the beaten track, overlooking a small, calm, slightly stony beach. Huts from 60 baht per night.

Thong Sai Bay

Moving further around the island, we come to this bay, situated on the absolute peninsula.

Imperial Hotel One of two on the island belonging to the

Imperial Hotel group. A luxury hotel, with all the usual services and extras to be expected, including: swimming pool, TV and video room, live entertainment, fully equipped restaurant and pick-up service from town. Situated on a secluded part of the beach. Single studio from 4329 baht per night. The honeymoon suite available from 5439 baht per night. The hotel, as the prices suggest, is strictly up-market. Restaurant prices also reflect this. Bookings can be make in Bangkok (Tel: 02 254 0023-100).

Choengmon Bay

Another small, secluded bay, with white, powdery sands and calm, crystal clear water, this is in our opinion one of the prettiest beaches on the island.

Choengmon Bungalows Basic bungalows, with no fan or shower, from 50 baht per night. Cabins with separate shower and toilet but no fan at 100 baht. Quite large wooden bungalows, with bathroom, toilet and fan for 250 and 300 baht. Pretty good value. There is also a small shop for groceries, a travel agent, motorbike hire and a table-tennis table.

Choengmon Village (Tel: 02 212 1545) This place boasts one hundred and twenty rooms, all nicely furnished and with verandah and modern bathroom. Four different types of bungalow accommodation available. Standard single with fan is 700 baht; standard double with fan is 800 baht. Superior single with fan is 1000 baht; superior double with fan is 1200 baht. Additional charge of 200 baht for an extra bed.

P S Village Has pretty large wooden style bungalows, from 50 baht for basic, 80 baht with toilet, 300 and 350 baht with shower, toilet and fan.

Chatkaeo Resort Six bungalows at 150 baht, and six slightly bigger and better at 250 baht. Fan included in all bungalows. Cheap menu here.

Island View The last set of bungalows on this beach, on the corner of this part of the island, looking out on Koh Fan Yai, a tiny island which can be reached on foot at low tide. There is a small bar at this point, pleasantly situated amongst the pine trees. Bungalows start at 50 baht for basic, no fan, going up to 100 baht with fan, and 250 baht with shower, toilet and fan. Motorbikes can be rented.

Coral Bay Resort (Tel: 077 272 222, 273 213 ext. 201) Situated a couple of kilometres round the track after leaving Choeng Mon, this is located at Yai Noi Bay, at the top northern end of Chaweng Beach. It has a total of forty-two bungalows of the raised wooden type; very spacious and clean. Each has a large balcony with beach view, bathroom with hot and cold water, and air conditioning or ceiling fan. Extras include: restaurant and bar serving Thai, Chinese and European food, swimming pool, video room, traditional Thai massage, jeep and motorbike hire. Prices for accommodation are 1300 and 1450 baht per night. Geared for the holiday-maker, with hotel-like facilities.

Chaweng Beach

This extensive beach has a wealth of bungalows of varying price and style. It offers peace and quiet at the northern end, and plenty of bars and night life at the other. We list here a variety of accommodations to suit all types, but there are many more available from which to choose (see page 8).

O P Bungalows A nice Chinese resort, situated pretty high up the beach, overlooking the tiny island of Matlang. Accommodation includes toilet, shower and fan, and is quite competitively priced at 200 baht per night for fairly large rooms. The view from here is beautiful. Chinese and Thai food available.

Samui Cabana (Tel: 077 421 405) Has forty bungalows, with fan, shower and toilet. Nice and clean, quite large rooms. Single rooms start at 350 baht; doubles at 400 baht; twin rooms with sea view from 600 baht. Nice raised bar and a good restaurant. Overseas calls can be made here.

The Island (Tel: 077 421 313) This has a variety of bungalows of brick and wood. Recently rebuilt, this place offers an excellent service, with an efficiently run restaurant serving Western and Thai cuisine, and an outstanding bar offering all sorts of concoctions and cocktails. Single rooms with fans start at 150 baht, going up to doubles at 350 baht.

Larger bungalows are 600 baht, and extra large, air-conditioned seafront bungalows are 1500 baht. All accommodation is fully furnished, and a daily cleaning service is provided. Long-term stayers can try for a discount here.

Lotus Offers furnished, brick chalet style bungalows from 250 baht, with Western toilet and shower. Good value, with excellent breakfast and home-made bread.

Suneast Bungalows Good-sized accommodation, with fan and separate toilet and shower. Starts at 200 baht per night. 250 and 400 baht gets you a chalet-type place. Excellent food.

Coconut Grove Has old wooden bungalows, with shower, toilet and fan, overlooking the beach, from 80 baht. They also have newer bungalows at 150 baht and chalet-type accommodation at 200 and 250 baht per night. Very friendly atmosphere here.

Best Beach Bungalows with fan are 50 baht. With toilet and shower, 150 baht, up to 250 baht. Good food.

Malibu Offers good, clean bungalows with shower and fan, from 100 up to 250 baht. Windsurfers and a catamaran can be hired at a daily or hourly rate.

Thai Garden Really cheap bungalows, some overlooking the sea, in quite a nice setting. A number of huts available at 50 baht.

The White House Furnished, clean rooms, in a garden setting. Standard single rooms with fan, 1000 baht. Standard double with fan, 1100 baht. Superior single with air conditioning 1200 baht. Superior double with air conditioning 1300 baht. Beach-front bungalows with air conditioning 1500 baht. Deluxe with air conditioning, 1800 baht. Additional beds, 200 baht extra. In high seasons (15 July to 31 August and 20 December to 10 January) add an extra 100 baht per night per bungalow. No charge for children under twelve years old sharing the same bungalow as the parents.

The Village Situated a little further down the beach, and owned by the same people as The White House. The garden setting is rather nicely done here, and the prices are the same as at The White House, but there are also family suites with air conditioning available at 1500 baht and 1700 baht on the beach front. Geared towards the holiday-maker.

The Pansea (Tel: 077 421 384) Has very roomy and nicely

furnished wooden bungalows, very clean and comfortable. Caters for an up-market clientele, with a Western-style restaurant, serving lunch at 220 baht and dinner at over 330 baht per person. Accommodation is referred to as "cottages" and comprises one large room with separate bathroom, shower and toilet, one king-size bed and one standard bed, all with air conditioning and a private terrace. Can sleep three adults, or two adults and two children. Prices vary according to season, ranging from 1800 to 2100 baht per cottage. Special buffet laid on every Saturday, which is a three-course meal at 450 baht per person. Thai boxing exhibitions and traditional Thai dancing shows held quite regularly to entertain their clients. Amenities for sailing and windsurfing.

First Bungalows Depending on which way you approach, this is either at the top end of Chaweng Beach, or at the beginning, hence its name. It is also at the beginning of Chaweng Noi Beach (Little Chaweng). There is a great bar built on the rocks overlooking Chaweng Beach. Bungalows are many and varied, ranging from as little as 80 baht; these ones however are pretty hard to get, as they are normally occupied by long-termers. There are also wooden and brick chalet-type bungalows from 150 up to 500 baht. Well stocked supermarket and a travel agent.

Maeo Further up Chaweng Noi. Basic huts with just a bed for 50 baht. Bungalows with shower, toilet and fan 150 and 200 baht. Cheap and varied menu selection.

Lamai

Along the 4169 road towards Lamai are several bungalows, built on the rocks overlooking Coral Bay. In fact three of the resorts there are called Coral Cove, the nicest, in our opinion, being the one listed. (See also list on page 8.)

Coral Cove Reggae Café Set high in the rocks, with great views. Basic huts at 50 baht. More comfortable bungalows with fan, separate shower, toilet and a fairly large balcony cost 150 and 200 baht. Motorbike hire and snorkelling equipment available.

Golden Cliff Resort (Tel: 077 421 409) Further along the 4169 and built off the beach, above the road at Thong Ta

Kien Bay, this place offers fairly new bungalows, with single rooms with fan at 300 baht, double rooms with fan at 400 baht. Just about to be constructed are a further fifteen air-conditioned rooms. All huts are spacious and clean with balconies offering a sea view. Overseas telephone calls can be made here.

Island Resort At the beginning of Lamai Beach, from the Chaweng end, this sits on a quiet beach. Bungalows with shower and toilet are 100 and 150 baht. Quite good value and very spacious. Look out for the Montana Saloon, run by two American "gentlemen".

Weekenden Villa Bungalows at 150 baht and a good cheap menu. Tours and special trips organised here.

The beach town of Lamai is fast becoming a tourist trap, and the abundance of bars and restaurants of all kinds means that most nationalities will find something to suit their tastes, although at the moment, there are not enough people around to fill them, and most places appear pretty empty. There are also plenty of "girlie" bars for lonely men. Here also can be found the Flamingo Disco, open every night, playing mostly pop and disco music, and occasionally holding Thai boxing exhibitions. Bungalow prices tend to be a touch dearer.

Marina Bungalows Raised wooden style bungalows, with large balconies, at 200 and 250 baht.

Mira Mare Bungalows at 150 baht. Currently more are being built. This is an unsheltered spot of no great attraction. Water skis can be rented.

Sea Breeze Has some older style wooden bungalows at 150 baht. Also some newer, brick type, at 200, 250 and 350 baht.

Casanova's Bungalows Next to Sea Breeze, with rooms 100 and 150 baht. Also has a swimming pool.

Hinta Hinyai

Signposted a little further along the road, this is not another town or village, as you might expect, but a small dirt road which leads to a tiny beach where there are some huge boulders you can sit on; here also are the famous Grandfather and Grandmother rock formations.

Noi Bungalows Next to Hinta Hinyai: fairly peaceful, with a good sea view. Bungalows here from a very modest 80 baht for a basic share shower situation to 250 baht for accommodation with better facilities.

Between Noi Bungalows and the beginning of South Lamai beach are about half a dozen sets of bungalows which we know of, but did not get the change to try out. Prices are in the popular 150 to 250 baht region, but there is no beach here. Good snorkelling, but very little else.

South Lamai

The Hilton Garden Resort Brand new, situated on a particularly lovely stretch of white sand on the South Lamai beach. As its name implies, the owners have tried their best to make it a resort with lots to do; its facilities include: a large swimming pool with slides and springboards, a billiards room, and a fully equipped, Western-style workout gymnasium. Brick built chalets, laid out in rather too much of a regimented style for our tastes around the activity building, are fully equipped with modern conveniences. Great for those visitors who prefer comfort to authenticity. Prices start at 400 baht for a very comfortable double bungalow, up to 600 baht for the added convenience of air conditioning. There is also a shop and restaurant, and motorbike and jeep hire is available.

Samui Orchid Resort Sits on fifteen acres of coconut plantation, two kilometres from the main road down to the white sand beach. A new resort, providing non-detached brick built chalets in a garden setting, and some detached, thatched bungalows. All equipped with modern facilities. Ranging from 450 baht with a fan to 750 to 1000 baht for the deluxe variety. Also has a large swimming pool overlooking the beach and a thatched, bamboo-built restaurant with Thai and Western cuisine. The sea here is particularly good for snorkelling, as the coral reef stretches the whole way along the beach. Snorkelling equipment hire available.

Laem Set Inn Further south, set on a very small, clean white sand beach. Particularly peaceful, and well off the beaten track, it has a pretty and comfortable open-air lounge and library, a swimming pool, international tele- phone facilities, and the only two-storey bungalows we came across. Even though we thought this place one of the most aesthetically pleasing that we visited, we found the 850 baht charged just a bit too steep for the type of accom- modation offered. Definitely a place for the "early to bed, early to rise" lifestyle.

Ban Kao Bay

River Garden Bungalows Further south again, with old Samui-style, small wooden bungalows without shower or fan, at 100 to 150 baht. The beach is not particularly good here.

Diamond Restaurant Just a walk from River Garden Bungalows, situated on the Ban Kao Beach, with bungalows reasonably priced at 60 baht and 80 baht with shower. A good spot.

Waikiki Bungalows The next to appear along the beach road. Fairly new-looking brick built chalet style accommo- dation with fan for 200 baht.

Phang Ka Bay

This bay is reached by travelling around the southwest tip of the island.

Emerald Cove Bungalows Yet another very peaceful resting place, with the added attraction of being one of the best spots from which to watch the sunset. Good value bungalows, reasonably priced from 50 to 80 baht for the smaller ones with basic shower and fan, up to 150 baht for larger accommodation with basic shower and fan, but more space and a better view.

Pearl Bay Bungalows A variety of types of accommoda- tion, from 60, 80 and 100 baht with shower and toilet, up to 180 baht for a place with two big beds and the bathroom facility.

Seagull Bungalows Small cheap bungalows for 80 baht with shower, 100 baht for larger ones with private bathroom.

Vastervik Bungalows and Restaurant A little further northwards along the beach, towards Naton. Can also be reached by taking a side turning off the main island road. Swedish owned and very comfortable. The friendly owner offers dormitory accommodation for 50 baht a night in fairly spacious rooms with a fan, with a very clean, modern bathroom and toilet conveniently close. Rooms also available at 200 and 300 baht. This is a great spot from which to view the sunset, and the restaurant sits right on the beach, providing Swedish, Thai and other Western dishes. Fishing trips, diving and snorkelling are all easily organised from here, too.

Useful addresses

Airlines, Bangkok

Aeroflot Soviet Airlines, 7 Silom Road. Tel: 233-6965/7.
Air France, 3 Patpong Road. Tel: 236-9279/90.
Air Lomka, 1 Patpong Road. Tel: 236-9292/3.
British Airways, 2nd Floor Chan Issara Tower, Rama IV
  Road. Tel: 236-8655.
Burma Airways, 208 Surawongse Road. Tel: 234-9692.
Cathay Pacific Airways, 109 Surawongse Road. Tel:
  235-6022/6, 233-6105.
C A A C, 143/1-2 Rama IV Road. Tel: 235-6510/1,
  235-1880.
China Airways, Siam Centre, Ramal Road.
  Tel: 251-9656/9, 251-9750.
Garuda, 944/19 Rama IV Road. Tel: 233-3873.
Japan Airlines, 1 Patpong Road. Tel: 234-9105/18.
KLM Royal Dutch Airlines, 2 Patpong Road.
  Tel: 235-5150/9.
Korean Airlines, Dusit Thani Hotel, Rama IV Road.
  Tel: 234-9283.
Lufthansa German Airlines, 331/1-3 Silom Road.
  Tel: 234-1350/9.
Malaysian Airlines System, 98/102 Surawongse Road.
  Tel: 234-9790/4, 234-9795/9.
Philippine Airlines, 1-3 Floor Chongkolnee Building,
  Aurawongse Road. Tel: 233-2350/2.
Quantas Airways, 14-8 Patpong Road. Tel: 236-0102.
Royal Nepal Airlines, 1/4 Convent Road. Tel: 233-2921/4.

SAS Scandinavian Airlines System, 312 Ramal Road.
Tel: 236-0303.
Singapore Airlines, 2 Silom Road. Tel: 236-0303.
Swissair Transport, 1 Silom Road. Tel: 233-2931.
Thai Airways Co Ltd (Domestic), 6 Larn Luang Road.
Tel: 531-0022, 280-0070.
Thai Airways International, 89 Vibhavadi-Rangsit Road.
Tel: 523-6121, 513-0121.

Embassies

Thai Embassy (UK), 30 Queens Gate, London SW7 5JB.
Tel: 071-589 0173.
Tourist Authority of Thailand (T A T), Rajadamnoen Nok
Avenue, Bangkok. (Head Office) Tel: 282-1143/5.
Tourist Authority of Thailand (T A T), Sala Prachakom,
Na Muang Road, Surat Thani. Tel: 077 282-422,
077 282-424.

Surat Thani

Bus terminal 273-840/1.
Police station 272-095.
Post office 272-013.
Railway station 311-213.
Tourist police 282-829.

Hospitals

Surat Thani 272-331.
Ban Don 272-767.

APPENDIX 3

Useful words and phrases

Unfortunately for the likes of us poor Westerners, the Thai language depends largely upon the tone of voice used rather than the actual words spoken, so you may find your attempts meet with great amusement. But do not be disheartened — a Thai often shows appreciation through laughter. Listen carefully, and you will soon pick up a few useful sentences. English is widely spoken and is taught in schools on the island. A few Samuians speak German but this language is more widely spoken in Phuket or Pattaya.

To be polite, the male speaker will end his sentence with *khrap* while the female will use the work *kha*. These two words can also be used to denote agreement or "yes". The following list contains just a few basic words and phrases which may help you get by.

Good day/Hello	*Sawat dii khrap/kha*
Goodbye	*La kom khrap/kha*
Please	*Proad*
Thank you	*Khawp khun khrap/kha*
Can you help me?	*Chaii chun noi dai mai?*
I don't understand	*Chun mai kao chai*
Slow down	*Cha cha*
Stop	*Yud*
I am sorry	*Chun sia chai*
What is your name?	*Khun cheu! arai*
How are you?	*Pen hangai?*
I am fine	*Sabaay dii* (This phrase may also be used as the question "how are you?")
No	*Mai*

Where is?	*Yuu thii! Mai?*
Bathroom	*Hawng! nam!*
Toilet	*Hawng! suam!*
Hotel	*Rohng raem*
Station	*Sathaa nii*
Post Office	*Praisanii*
When?	*Mua rai?*
Today	*Wan nii*
Tomorrow	*Prung nii*
Yesterday	*Meua! waan*
How much?	*Thad! rai*
Too expensive	*Phaeng pai*
Cheap	*Thuuk* (use only when selling!)
It doesn't matter	*Mai! pen rai khrap/kha*
Very good	*De mark*
A little	*Nit nawy*
Rice	*Khao!*
Marker	*Talad*
Bus Terminal	*Bor kor sor*

Counting

1	*Nwung*	11	*Sip et*
2	*Sawng*	12	*Sip sawng*
3	*Saam*	13	*Sip saam*
4	*Sii*	14	*Sip sii*
5	*Haa*	20	*Yii sip*
6	*Hok*	21	*Yii sip et*
7	*Jet*	22	*Yii sip sawng*
8	*Paet*	30	*Saam sip*
9	*Kao*	40	*Sii sip*
10	*Sip*	50	*Haa sip*
100	*Neung rawy*	200	*Sawng rawy*

Index

accommodation 25-6,
  67-78
air services and air-
  lines 13-14, 15, 79-80
airport 14
Ang Thong Marine National
  park 44

Baan Khaay 59
Ban Kao Bay
  accommodation 77
Ban Sa Ket 46
Ban Taling Ngam 46
Ban Thale 46
Ban Tong Tanot 46
Bang Kao 45
Bangkok
  air services and
    airlines 13, 79-80
  buses and coaches 15-16
  embassies 80
  rail services 15
  travel agents 16
banks 12
bars 33-4
Big Buddha (beach) 41
  accommodation 69-70
Big Buddha Wat 45, 51
Bo Phut 41, 51
  accommodation 68-9
Bottle Beach 59
Buddhism 18-19
buffalo fighting 54-5
bungalows 25-6
buses and coaches
  mainland 15-16

Chalok Lum 58
Chaweng beach 40
  accommodation 72-4

children 63
Choengmon Bay
  accommodation 71-2
climate 10
clothing 10
coaches see buses and
  coaches
cockighting 55
Coral Cove 51
credit cards 12
currency 11-12
customs (local) 20-1
cycling 50-1

diving and diving
  courses 51
doctors and dentists
  37, 62
Don Sak 14
dressmakers 38
drinks 32-3
drugs 61

embassies 80

ferries 14, 15
festivals 21
first-aid kit 10-11
fishing trips 52, 55-6
food 27-9
fruit 29

Grandmother and Grand-
  father rocks 46, 51

Haadrin Beach 59
Hat Thong Yang 41
health precautions 61-2
Hin Lad Waterfall 43, 50
Hinta Hinyai 46

accommodation 75-6
historical background 17
hospitals 62, 80
Hua Thanon 46

immigration office 37
islanders 18

jeep hire 23

Koh Fau 51
Koh Katen 46
Koh Matlang 56
Koh Mudson 46
Koh Phangan 58-9
Koh Tan 46
Koh Tao 51, 59-60

Lamai 41, 50
  accommodation 74-5

Mae Haad 59
Mae Nam 41
  accommodation 67-8
Mah Koh (island) 9
markets 37
massage 56-7
medical services 62
meditation and meditation
  courses 48
Mekong whisky 32
monasteries 45
money 11-12
motorbike hire 22-4
museums 49

Na-Muang Waterfall 43-4,
  50
Naton 9, 35-9
  accommodation 38-9, 67

Pangan (island) 9

passports 11
petrol stations 24, 37
Phang Ka Bay
  accommodation 77-8
postal services 35

rail services main-
  land 15
religions 18-20
restaurants 29-32, 38, 46
roads 9

Samui Highland Park 44
sea and tides 41-2
seafood 31-2, 38
shopping 37-8
Silangu 49
snooker 56
snorkelling and
  snorkelling courses 51-2
Songkran Festival 21
South Lamai
  accommodation 76-7
sunburn 63
Surat Thani
  air services 15
  buses 16, 80
  embassies 80
  ferries 14
  rail services 15
  other services - telephone
    numbers 80

Ta Loy (island) 9
Ta Pao (island) 9
tailors 38
Tan (island) 9
Tao (island) 9
tax and tax clearance 65-6
taxis 22
Thai boxing 52-4
Thai embassy

(London) 11, 80
Thai language 81-2
Thai specialities (food) 28
Thong Sala 58
Thong Sai Bay
  accommodation 70-1
Thong Son Bay
  accommodation 70
Thong Thaa Paan Beach 59
time 64
tipping 12
Tong Yang Bay 44
tourist police station 35

tourist season 10
travel agents, Bangkok 16

vaccinations 61
vehicle hire 22-4
visas and visa renewal
  11, 64-5
vocabulary 81-2

Wat Laem Saw 45
Wat Pangbua 48
water 62
water sports 42